The Crash of 1929

Other books in the At Issue in History series:

The Attack on Pearl Harbor
The Conquest of the New World
The Indian Reservation System
Japanese American Internment Camps
The Nuremberg Trials
The Sinking of the Titanic
The Treaty of Versailles

The Crash
of 1929

Louise I. Gerdes, *Book Editor*

Daniel Leone, *President*
Bonnie Szumski, *Publisher*
Scott Barbour, *Managing Editor*

OPPOSING
VIEWPOINTS®
SERIES

AT ISSUE IN HISTORY

Greenhaven Press, Inc.
San Diego, California

Library of Congress Cataloging-in-Publication Data

The crash of 1929 / Louise I. Gerdes, book editor.
    p.   cm. — (At issue in history)
    Includes bibliographical references and index.
    ISBN 0-7377-0818-2 (pbk. : alk. paper) —
    ISBN 0-7377-0819-0 (lib. : alk. paper)
    1. Depressions—1929. 2. Depressions—1929—United
States. 3. Stock Market Crash, 1929. 4. New York Stock
Exchange—History. 5. United States—Economic conditions—
1918–1945. I. Gerdes, Louise I. II. Series.
        highlighting 3-09
  HB3717 1929 .C73 2002
  338.5'4'097309043—dc21
                                                    2001040342

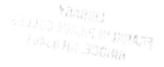

Cover photo: Corbis
Library of Congress, 15

© 2002 by Greenhaven Press, Inc.
10911 Technology Place, San Diego, CA 92127

Printed in the U.S.A.

Contents

Chapter 1: The Great Bull Market

Chapter 2: The Panic on Wall Street

Chapter 3: The Aftermath

quickly, hoping to restore confidence after the crash, the market continued to drop, and tales of corruption and excess transformed speculators from heroes into villains. While some scholars blame the crash on the greed of speculators, others fault capitalism and diverse economic factors.

Foreword

Historian Robert Weiss defines history simply as "a record and interpretation of past events." Both elements—record and interpretation—are necessary, Weiss argues.

> Names, dates, places, and events are the essence of history. But historical writing is not a compendium of facts. It consists of facts placed in a sequence to tell a connected story. A work of history is not merely a story, however. It also must analyze what happened and *why*—that is, it must interpret the past for the reader.

For example, the events of December 7, 1941, that led President Franklin D. Roosevelt to call it "a date which will live in infamy" are fairly well known and straightforward. A force of Japanese planes and submarines launched a torpedo and bombing attack on American military targets in Pearl Harbor, Hawaii. The surprise assault sank five battleships, disabled or sank fourteen additional ships, and left almost twenty-four hundred American soldiers and sailors dead. On the following day, the United States formally entered World War II when Congress declared war on Japan.

These facts and consequences were almost immediately communicated to the American people who heard reports about Pearl Harbor and President Roosevelt's response on the radio. All realized that this was an important and pivotal event in American and world history. Yet the news from Pearl Harbor raised many unanswered questions. Why did Japan decide to launch such an offensive? Why were the attackers so successful in catching America by surprise? What did the attack reveal about the two nations, their people, and their leadership? What were its causes, and what were its effects? Political leaders, academic historians, and students look to learn the basic facts of historical events and to read the intepretations of these events by many different sources, both primary and secondary, in order to develop a more complete picture of the event in a historical context.

In the case of Pearl Harbor, several important questions surrounding the event remain in dispute, most notably the role of President Roosevelt. Some historians have blamed his policies for deliberately provoking Japan to attack in order to propel America into World War II; a few have gone so far as to accuse him of knowing of the impending attack but not informing others. Other historians, examining the same event, have exonerated the president of such charges, arguing that the historical evidence does not support such a theory.

The Greenhaven At Issue in History series recognizes that many important historical events have been interpreted differently and in some cases remain shrouded in controversy. Each volume features a collection of articles that focus on a topic that has sparked controversy among eyewitnesses, contemporary observers, and historians. An introductory essay sets the stage for each topic by presenting background and context. Several chapters then examine different facets of the subject at hand with readings chosen for their diversity of opinion. Each selection is preceded by a summary of the author's main points and conclusions. A bibliography is included for those students interested in pursuing further research. An annotated table of contents and thorough index help readers to quickly locate material of interest. Taken together, the contents of each of the volumes in the Greenhaven At Issue in History series will help students become more discriminating and thoughtful readers of history.

Introduction:
The Lessons of
the Crash of 1929

On "Black Tuesday," October 29, 1929, a total of 16,410,030 shares of stock were traded on the floor of the New York Stock Exchange; in the next few weeks, more than $30 billion disappeared from the American economy. The stock market had hit an unprecedented low. Thousands of investors, including ordinary working people, were financially ruined. Banks that had speculated with their depositors' money were wiped out. Because many Americans at that time viewed the stock market as the chief indicator of the nation's financial strength, public confidence in the economy was shattered. When the final bell rang that black day in October, fortunes were lost, careers ruined, and hopes dashed. The nation's economic outlook was bleak.

One of the harsh realities of high finance is that business runs in cycles. Recessions, depressions, and stock market panics are inevitable, so why do people continue to be interested in a stock market crash that occurred more than seventy years ago? Had the Crash of 1929 not been followed by a devastating depression that permeated the lives of most Americans for an entire decade, the subject might be of interest only to speculators and students of finance, but the Great Depression that followed the crash forever marked the lives of those who lived through the 1930s. Although most scholars agree that the Crash of 1929 did not cause the Great Depression, historian Tom Shachtman remarks that the crash was "the beginning of a new kind of necessary consciousness, the beginning of a modernity unalloyed by both the wonderful simplicity and the obvious imperfections of an older and earlier American civilization. The crash was a time of instant change—not the cause of the change, but simply the moment when it happened."[1] Scholars who seek to understand the social and cultural changes that followed

11

the crash see it as a turning point—a symbol of a radical shift in American perspective and attitudes.

Prelude to Disaster

To understand why the Crash of 1929 marked such a radical shift in American attitudes, most scholars begin by examining the era of prosperity that preceded the crash. The "Roaring Twenties" began just after World War I, when most Americans tried to cast off the horrors and wartime shortages of that tragic period. The United States experienced an era of unparalleled prosperity during the 1920s; the country had emerged from World War I as a creditor nation, and the nation's productivity and economic growth were unprecedented. The gross national product grew at an annual rate of 4.7 percent from 1922 to 1929, unemployment averaged only 3.7 percent, industrial output increased by more than 60 percent for the decade, and the average annual income rose significantly from $520 to $681.

Authorities generally agree that technology played a large part in the economic boom of the twenties. Not only did Americans have more money to spend, but growing application of electricity in manufacturing gave consumers a choice of new and affordable products such as phonographs, washing machines, vacuum cleaners, telephones, sewing machines, and radios. Before the autumn of 1920, Americans had never heard of radio broadcasting, but by 1922, radio was the latest craze. By 1929, Americans spent almost 1 percent of national income on radios.

If any object, however, was a symbol of American prosperity in the 1920s, it was the automobile. Henry Ford's assembly-line techniques not only provided assembly-line workers with higher wages but made automobiles available to new markets. When Ford began to use standardized, interchangeable parts and assembly-line techniques to build Model Ts in 1913, about 10 percent of American urban households owned cars. From 1919 to 1929 the number of cars more than tripled, and road construction boomed. According to Marci McDonald, "Almost single-handedly, Henry Ford turned car ownership into a national right. By 1929, 23.1 million Americans had bought an automobile."[2] To buy radios, cars, and other products, Americans turned to consumer credit, which had previously been stigmatized in American society. Finance companies proliferated, and between 1920 and 1929, installment buying quintupled to $6 billion.

The Great Bull Market

To many, the stock market of the Roaring Twenties represents the excesses of the era of prosperity. Investment in the stock market was no longer simply the province of bankers and financiers. The little guy could speculate with the seasoned pros in the pit. Americans bought not only cars and appliances, but stock on credit. Known as buying on margin, the stock buyer paid only a percentage, or margin, of the purchase price and borrowed the remainder from a broker, pledging the stock as collateral for the loan. This allowed even the luncheonette waitress and the shoeshine boy to invest in the stock market, and like the Charleston, stock speculation became the latest craze. It was fun, and many believed they could get rich like the flamboyant stock speculators, America's financial heroes.

During the latter years of the twenties, stock prices continued to rise and the Dow Jones Industrial Index reached record-breaking highs, with the market peaking in September 1929. Investors, caught up in the race to make a killing, invested their life savings, mortgaged their homes, and cashed in safer investments such as treasury bonds and bank accounts to get margin money. Billions of dollars were invested in the stock market as people began speculating on the rising stock prices.

While some believed the stock market would continue to rise and prosperity would continue indefinitely, others were not so optimistic and some even anticipated the coming crash. The headlines at the time reflected this contrast between optimism and pessimism. On October 16, 1929, *The New York Times* quoted economist Irving Fisher of Yale University and banker Charles E. Mitchell, who reassured investors that stocks would continue to rise, seeing no sign of a potential slump. In contrast, however, on September 6, 1929, *The New York Times* had cited business forecaster and statistician Roger Babson, who recommended that wise investors should pay up their loans and avoid trading on margin, predicting a looming crash. On October 2, 1929, the paper had quoted Craig B. Hazlewood, president of the American Bankers Association and vice president of First National Bank of Chicago, who warned that banks were overwhelmed by investment credit and suggested that banks that were eager to loan money were responsible for over-speculation. Hazlewood cautioned, "Many conservative bankers in this country are gravely alarmed over the mounting volume of credit that is being employed . . . both by brokers and by individuals."[3]

The market of late 1929 did show signs of trouble, and as news accounts at the time reveal, not everyone was blind to the dangers. The Federal Reserve Board, which oversees Federal Reserve banks, establishes monetary policy, including interest rates and credit, and monitors the economic health of the country, had been meeting every day behind closed doors as early as March 1929. On March 25, the market experienced the first of several minicrashes, creating a roller coaster market. During the summer of 1929, the market appeared to stabilize and on September 3, stock market prices peaked, but then the market began its final descent.

The Panic on Wall Street

The panic began on Thursday, October 24, 1929, when 12,894,650 shares changed hands on the New York Stock Exchange in a flood of sell orders. Unlike the immediate electronic transmission of stock transactions on today's market, the telegraphic ticker tape machine could not keep up with the trading that day, and issues were behind as much as one hour. Crowds began to gather outside the exchange, hoping to obtain news, and the police were called to control the masses of investors. After lunch, the market made a comeback and some of the big name company stocks recovered, but by the end of the day, the New York Stock Exchange had lost $4 billion, and it took exchange clerks until five o'clock the next morning to clear all of the transactions.

Trading on Friday and Saturday brought some relief and gave investors time to plan for what they knew would be a difficult week. On Monday, October 28, more than 9,250,000 shares were traded; unlike the previous Thursday, there was no dramatic recovery to offset losses. The next day, Tuesday, October 29, the market came crashing down. In the first few hours, stock prices fell so far and so fast that the gains of the previous year were wiped out. Frantic stockbrokers tried to call in margins, and panic-stricken investors liquidated their stocks, causing even more pressure on the market.

People gather outside of the New York Stock Exchange after the crash of October 24, 1929, now known as Black Thursday.

In the days that followed the crash, rumors ran rampant that people were jumping out of buildings in reaction to the crash. Comedian Eddie Cantor joked that a hotel clerk asked a guest registering for the penthouse suite if he wanted to rent it for sleeping or jumping. In reality, few committed suicide in the days that followed the crash, but the scandal that rocked the stock market and the banking industry in the months and years that followed the crash ruined the lives of many bankers and financial leaders. Some infamous speculators lived to regain their fortunes while others drifted into obscurity. The small speculators who invested on credit were called to restore their margin. Unable to meet the margin call, they became bankrupt overnight. These investors were forced to sell their belongings and even their homes to meet their debts.

Responding to the Crash

The day after the panic of Thursday, October 24, President Herbert Hoover, trying to restore confidence, remarked that "the fundamental business of the country, that is production and distribution of commodities, is on a sound and prosperous basis."[4] Hoover's reaction to the stock market crash was not surprising: Hoover encouraged optimism, arguing that pessimism would discourage investment and limit production. Although Hoover formed several conferences and commissions to study the nation's economic problems, he believed the government's role was merely to advise. He staunchly held to his ideals that the economy would correct itself without government interference. Historian Roger Biles summarizes Hoover's philosophy: "Hoover saw only failure in the heavy hand of coercive government, believing that America's history ratified the reliance of individual effort."[5]

Some historians argue that government inaction was the reason the initial recession turned into a prolonged depression. Hoover kept the Federal Reserve from expanding the money supply while bank panics and billions in lost deposits were depleting the money supply. Although Hoover did respond with some government action, most authorities maintain that it was too little too late. Hoover continued to sanction the creation of government agencies; however, their role was to remain advisory. While later generations have treated Hoover more kindly, his contemporaries condemned his performance.

Economists now generally agree there was no solution to the nation's financial problems, but at the time Hoover accepted complete responsibility. An angry and unkind American public was content to blame Herbert Hoover. People even named the communities of makeshift shacks erected at the outskirts of urban centers where displaced families were forced to live "Hoovervilles."

The End of an Era

Nineteenth-century values were crumbling, nineteenth-century American heroes along with them. Stock speculators no longer represented rugged individualism and American prosperity but corruption and greed, now blamed, along with Hoover, as the source of the nation's economic despair. American life had changed dramatically. When people began to lose their jobs, charity alone was insufficient to care for them, and whole communities came apart. Overcome with despair, many Americans reluctantly discarded their deeply held belief in self-reliance and turned to the federal government for assistance.

Unfortunately, these Americans looked to a government unfamiliar with the role of savior. No president had been asked to assume responsibility for managing the American economy. In the twenties, Americans expected the government to play only a minor role in their lives. This same government was now asked to create jobs, support farmers, protect investments, and insure the future security of its citizens. A government that had once focused primarily on foreign affairs was expected to protect American citizens from a domestic enemy more unfamiliar than any foreign foe it had ever faced.

Americans needed a strong paternal figure to lead them out of the depression; they found that figure in Franklin D. Roosevelt, who easily defeated Hoover for the presidency in 1932. Arguably no other president before or since has pushed the role of the executive branch to its limits like Roosevelt, who took on his paternal role openly and with the support of the people. Roosevelt made his objectives clear in his first inaugural address, delivered Saturday, March 4, 1933:

> In the event that the national emergency is still critical, I shall not evade the clear course of duty that will then confront me. I shall ask the Congress for the one remaining instrument to meet the crisis—broad Executive power to wage a war against the emergency, as great as the power that would be given me if we were in fact invaded by a foreign foe. . . . We do not distrust the future of essential democracy. The people of the United States have not failed. In their need they have registered a mandate that they want direct, vigorous action. They have asked for discipline and direction under leadership. They have made me the present instrument of their wishes. In the spirit of the gift I take it.[6]

The American people not only shifted their attitude toward the role of government after the crash, but also began to question traditional values and expectations. People who had once been preoccupied with how fast money could be made now wondered how they would survive. Cities that once functioned on the assumption that their inhabitants could support themselves now found that a substantial portion of the population could not find work. Parents who had hoped to pass their values on to their children now listened to their children speak disparagingly of their world. Those who had once looked to a hopeful future were now focused on the present, beset by fears of an unknown future. America was paying a price for its blind faith in limitless prosperity, and those who lived through the depression were forever changed by it. Shachtman writes, "These are changes in the American psyche; changes which, one can well argue, are permanent, cruel, and yet evidence of a more realistic attitude towards life."[7] Most Americans accepted responsibility for their financial condition and did what they could to survive.

Debating the Causes of the Crash

Economists and historians offer different explanations for what caused the Crash of 1929. The primary debate, however, is whether fundamental conditions or a speculative bubble drove the market upward, resulting in an inevitable crash. Although this debate will likely never be resolved, one of the most commonly accepted explanations of the 1929 boom and crash is forwarded by economists such as John Kenneth Galbraith, who argue that any event could have triggered irrational investors to sell, focusing on the inevitability of the bubble's collapse. When the stock market crashed, the individual stock speculator looked for someone to blame, but as Galbraith explains:

> No one was responsible for the great Wall Street crash. No one engineered the speculation that preceded it. Both were the product of the free choice and decision of hundreds of thousands of individuals. The latter were not led to the slaughter. They were impelled to it by the seminal lunacy which has always seized people who are seized in turn with the notion that they can become very rich.[8]

Other scholars, however, argue that many "fundamental" factors contributed to the economic decline that made the crash inevitable. Despite the wealth of prosperous individuals, most Americans were already poor, business had already begun to slow, and unemployment was increasing. Farmers had been overproducing crops at reduced value, and many farmers who had been caught up in the frenzy of purchasing farm mortgage options were hopelessly in debt. Savvy stock market manipulators had created massive holding companies by selling stocks and bonds and using the money to buy enough stock to control existing companies. When the stock market crashed, fewer customers were buying stocks and bonds, and the holding companies could not meet the huge interest payments on the bonds they had sold, so they too collapsed. Unfortunately, self-interest often translated into greed and abuse of economic liberty while competition failed to guarantee a free market. Certain individuals and firms began interfering with the economic freedom of others—large firms exploited small firms, monopolies controlled markets, public utilities exploited consumers, and competing employers pushed wages down.

Before the crash, some in government blamed the runaway stock speculation on the Federal Reserve Board. Hoover believed that the board failed to set a more conservative tone for banking. However, bankers believed that to curb speculation was as dangerous as to let it go unchecked. In fact, some say that Roy Young, governor of the Federal Reserve Board, was laughing as he watched the rising prices on the ticker tape. "What I am laughing at," he said, "is that I am sitting here trying to keep a hundred and twenty million people from doing what they want to do!"[9]

More than seventy years after the crash, economists and historians continue to debate what caused the crash and the Great Depression that followed. Moreover, scholars and speculators disagree whether a similar economic collapse can be predicted or prevented. Has America learned the lessons of the Crash of 1929? Perhaps humorist Will Rogers answered this question on November 17, 1929, when he concluded, "It takes years in this country to tell whether anybody's right or wrong. It's kinder a case of just how far ahead you can see. The fellow that can only see a week ahead is always the popular fellow, for he is looking with the crowd. But the one that can see years ahead, he has a telescope but he can't make anybody believe he has it."[10]

Notes

1. Tom Shachtman, *The Day America Crashed*. New York: G.P. Putnam's, 1979, p. 292.
2. Marci McDonald, "A History of Shopping Binges," *U.S. News & World Report*, May 24, 1999, p. 50.
3. Craig B. Hazlewood, "Hazlewood Warns Bankers on Credits," *The New York Times*, October 2, 1929, p. 5.

4. Quoted in Barry A. Wigmore, *The Crash and Its Aftermath: A History of Securities Markets in the United States, 1929–1933*. Westport, CT: Greenwood, 1985, p. 89.
5. Roger Biles, *A New Deal for the American People*. DeKalb: Northern Illinois University Press, 1991, p. 16.
6. Franklin D. Roosevelt, first inaugural address, Saturday, March 4, 1933. Taken from the Avalon Project at the Yale Law School: Documents in Law, History, and Diplomacy, available at www.yale.edu/lawweb/avalon/avalon.htm.
7. Shachtman, *The Day America Crashed*, p. 288.
8. John Kenneth Galbraith, *The Great Crash: 1929*. New York: Time, 1962, p. 4.
9. Quoted in Adrian A. Paradis, *The Hungry Years: The Story of the Great American Depression*. Philadelphia: Chilton, 1967, p. 21.
10. Will Rogers, *The Autobiography of Will Rogers*. Ed. Donald Day. Boston: Houghton Mifflin, 1929, p. 213.

Chapter 1

The Great Bull Market

1

The 1920s: A New Era of Prosperity

Thomas E. Hall and J. David Ferguson

The United States experienced a significant period of growth and prosperity in the 1920s, which resulted in an improved standard of living for many Americans, write Thomas E. Hall and J. David Ferguson, professors of economics at Miami University, in Oxford, Ohio. In the following excerpt from their book *The Great Depression: An International Disaster of Perverse Economic Policies*, Hall and Ferguson review the benefits that flowed from national prosperity and examine the reasons for the nation's economic growth. The author's explain, for example, that technological developments in production made the automobile accessible to middle-class Americans who then required gasoline, tires, and even roads to utilize their vehicles. This, in turn, stimulated ancillary industries such as petroleum that provided these products. The authors note, however, that those with higher incomes were experiencing the benefits of national prosperity to a greater degree than those with lower incomes. Hall and Ferguson also point out that many were concerned about the potential pitfalls of sudden economic growth, noting the startling rise in stock prices and the collateral boom in stock speculation that seemed to consume many Americans who had extra cash.

The 1920s were a period of significant prosperity in the United States. From the end of the recession in July 1921 to the economic peak in August 1929 that preceded the Great Depression, economic output growth averaged

Adapted from excerpts of *The Great Depression: An International Disaster of Perverse Economic Policies*, by Thomas E. Hall and J. David Ferguson. Copyright © by the University of Michigan 1998. Reprinted by permission of the University of Michigan Press.

5.9 percent per year, and that figure includes output declines during two mild recessions that occurred in 1923–24 and 1926–27. This economic growth is quite remarkable when one considers that the long-run average growth rate of the U.S. economy is around 3.0 percent per year.

An Improved Standard of Living

This vibrant growth was associated with rapid improvements in living standards for urban Americans. This was the time when many middle-class Americans obtained automobiles, electrical appliances, and their own houses. [Historian Jim] Potter notes that during the 1920s the number of residences rose 25 percent, telephones increased 54 percent, food production went up about 50 percent, the number of automobiles registered went from 9 million in 1920 to 23 million in 1929, kilowatt-hours of electricity generated more than doubled, and there were enormous increases in sales of electrical cooking devices, vacuums, and radios (1974). At the same time, consumption of education and recreational services boomed as well. Potter contends that the decade "amounted to a massive increase in consumption, perhaps greater in total and *per capita* than in any previous decade in American history" (1974).

The output gains of the 1920s were associated with mild deflation as the Gross National Product (GNP) deflator fell at an average annual rate of 0.5 percent from 1921 to 1929. In other words, the aggregate supply schedule was shifting to the right more rapidly than the aggregate demand schedule was.* The major source of the rapid growth of aggregate supply was widespread application of assembly-line techniques in several industries including household appliances, food processing, and tobacco. The resulting productivity gains were such that while total employment in manufacturing was roughly constant from 1920 to 1929, output grew over 60 percent.

The increased ownership and use of autos was an important stimulus to growth. In fact, it is difficult to overstate the role of the automobile in helping to generate the economic gains of the 1920s. Thanks to the cost reductions resulting

---

*Aggregate supply is the total production of goods and services available at a range of prices, during a given time period. Aggregate demand is the total real expenditures on goods and services produced that buyers are willing and able to make at different price levels, during a given time period.

from the application of modern mass production techniques by Ford Motor Company in 1913, retail prices for the Model T fell from $950 per auto in 1908 to $290 by 1924. At such prices a Model T (and many other competing models) became affordable for middle-class families. As a result, auto ownership rose significantly during the 1910s and through the 1920s. At the same time, many roads were being paved, which stimulated the use of the autos. From 1920 through 1929 the number of miles of surface roads nearly doubled from 388,000 to 626,000. The resulting increase in both the number of automobiles and their use generated a massive stimulus to the demand for complementary goods and services. The petroleum industry boomed, as did the production of tires, traffic signals, service stations, and everything else associated with auto use at that time. Experience gained in these growing industries likely resulted in more efficient production techniques and improving productivity. . . .

Investment spending boomed during the decade as well. Of special note was the enormous rise in spending on both business and residential structures. Investment in business structures peaked at roughly equal values in both 1925 and 1929, and these inflation-adjusted levels were not reached again until 1953. Residential construction peaked in 1928 at inflation-adjusted levels not reattained until 1947.

What factors contributed to the construction boom of the 1920s? The residential construction boom was certainly partly to satisfy pent-up demand generated by low building rates during and shortly after World War I. During the war resources were diverted toward military uses, and then immediately after the war mortgage financing was difficult to obtain. When financing finally became readily available, home building boomed. The automobile, too, was important, because it allowed people to move to outlying areas where the first big subdivisions were being built. Yet another factor was the building cycle of 18 to 22 years, which was based on cycles in population growth. A peak in this cycle was apparently hit during the mid-1920s. Finally, several investigators have claimed that the housing market had a speculative element to it that resulted in an overbuilt market by the late 1920s. For example, [historians and economists] Ben Bolch, Fels Rendigs, and Marshall McMahon contend that speculative overbuilding is demonstrated by the fact that from 1918 to 1926 net household formation exceeded housing starts, while from 1926 to 1929 housing starts exceeded net household formation (1971). Robert J. Gordon and John M. Veitch argue that a speculative element is demonstrated by the fact that from 1924 to 1927 the ratio of residential construction to GNP was "by far its highest level of the twentieth century" (1986). Alexander James Field points out that optimistic entrepreneurs were so busy subdividing acreage into building lots during the 1920s that after the crash in home building America was awash in vacant building lots: "In New Jersey alone . . . [there was] enough prematurely subdivided acreage in 1936 to supply over a million 6,000-square-foot lots, one for every family then resident in the state" (1992). It was also estimated that nationally there were roughly as many vacant building lots as there were occupied homes.

This was the time when many middle-class Americans obtained automobiles, electrical appliances, and their own houses.

A similar boom occurred in business structures. Much of this construction was of office buildings as the growth of large firms required larger buildings to house their employees. At the same time, the development of safe and reliable elevators allowed far taller buildings to be built than had been built before. So in cities, especially New York, many very large office buildings were built, the Empire State Building being the outstanding example. Another factor in the nonresidential construction boom was the building of electrical generating plants to help meet the increasing demand for electricity in urban areas.

Government purchases were stimulative at the state and local level, but at the federal level spending in 1929 was below the level of 1921. A good part of state and local spending went for road construction to meet the increased demand caused by the proliferation of automobiles, as well as for sewer construction in the expanding residential areas.

Dark Clouds on the Horizon

In the midst of this 1920s prosperity were two features that many argue were dark clouds on the horizon: the worsening distribution of income and the stock market boom. The distribution-of-income problem refers to the fact that while most people were becoming better off, those at the top of the income scale were becoming relatively much more affluent than those in lower income brackets. For example, Johnathan Hughes cites figures showing that the share of total income accruing to the top 1.0 percent of income earners rose from 12 percent in 1922 to 13.7 percent in 1929 (1987). Over that same period, the share of wealth held by the top 1 percent of adults rose from 32 percent to 38 percent. In 1922 the top 1 percent of income recipients accounted for 49 percent of total U.S. saving; by 1929 they accounted for 80 percent of saving. Jeffrey Williamson and Peter H. Lindert report that using any of a number of measures of income inequality, the period of 1928 and the first three quarters of 1929 may include one of "the highest income inequalities in American history" (1980).

Williamson and Lindert contend that the cause of this increased income inequality was the high rate of unbalanced technological progress during the period, that is, laborsaving technological innovations that favored one group of workers over another (1980). During the 1920s, laborsaving technological innovations were concentrated in manufacturing. This change caused a relative demand shift for labor, toward more skilled labor and away from unskilled labor. The laborsaving capital being put into use was replacing jobs at the unskilled level (assembly-line workers) while creating jobs at more skilled levels (for example, machine repairmen). Thus, wages of skilled workers rose relative to those of unskilled workers. Williamson and Lindert conclude that the technological progress during the 1920s raised the skilled labor wage premium by 0.98 percent per year (1980).

It is difficult to overstate the role of the automobile in helping to generate the economic gains of the 1920s.

Another important factor helping cause the changing distributions of income and wealth were the changes occurring in the functional distribution of income. Wages grew more slowly than output per worker, which suggests that corporate profits were rising. This change shows up as rising dividends, which constituted 4.3 percent of national income in 1920 and rose to 7.2 percent of national income by 1929. Since 82 percent of all dividends were paid to the top 5 percent of income earners, this clearly helped contribute to the change in income inequality. . . .

While most people were becoming better off, those at the top of the income scale were becoming relatively much more affluent than those in lower income brackets.

The second major problem in the minds of many was the stock market boom during the late 1920s. During much of the 1920s stock prices rose significantly, but especially during the last three years of the decade. Using Nathan S. Balke and Robert J. Gordon's (1986) index of common stock prices, equity values rose 27 percent in 1922, fell 7 percent in 1923, and then rose 16 percent in 1924, 27 percent in 1925, 5 percent in 1926, 25 percent in 1927, 29 percent in 1928, and finally another 30 percent during 1929 up to the peak in September. Certainly holding stocks during the 1920s was a good investment: if an individual had bought a representative basket of stocks at the economic trough in 1921 and had the sagacity to sell at the peak in September 1929 they would have earned a return of 412 percent *excluding dividend payments!* Furthermore, since the price level was falling slightly during that period, the real return would have been even higher.

According to several accounts, the stock market boom on Wall Street generated a great deal of excitement among Americans. While a relatively small number of people were directly involved in the market, only around 1.0 percent of the U.S. population according to John Kenneth Galbraith (1954), Americans got caught up in the mood of the times. Consider the comments of a major commentator of that era, the great social historian Frederick Lewis Allen:

> The speculative fever was infecting the whole country. Stories of fortunes made overnight were on everybody's lips. One financial commentator reported that

his doctor found patients talking about the market to the exclusion of everything else and that his barber was punctuating with the hot towel more than one account of the prospects of Montgomery Ward. Wives were asking their husbands why they were so slow, why they weren't getting in on all this, only to hear that their husbands had bought a hundred shares of American Linseed that very morning (1931).

Or what the noted historian William Leuchtenburg says about the market's effect on the general public:

> Even by the summer of 1929 the market had drawn people who never dreamed they would be caught in the speculative frenzy. How much longer could you hold out when your neighbor who bought General Motors at 99 in 1925 sold it at 212 in 1928? There were stories of a plunger who entered the market with a million dollars and ran it up to thirty millions in eight months, of a peddler who parlayed $4,000 into $250,000. The Bull Market was not simply a phenomenon of New York and Chicago; there were brokerage offices in towns like Steubenville, Ohio and Storm Lake, Iowa. Even non-investors followed the market news; like batting averages, it touched the statistical heart of the country. (1958)

2

"Everybody Ought to Be Rich": The Midsummer Boom

William K. Klingaman

The summer of 1929 represented the peak of America's prosperity during the 1920s, and while many believed the stock market would continue to climb indefinitely, others thought that the bubble must eventually burst. In the following excerpt from his book *1929: The Year of the Great Crash*, historian William K. Klingaman explores the activities of the stock market, its notorious speculators, and its critics during this momentous summer. For example, Klingaman tells the story of John J. Raskob, who extolled the virtues of stock speculation in his famous article "Everybody Ought to Be Rich," published in the August 1929 issue of *Ladies' Home Journal*. Raskob argued that with an investment of just fifteen dollars a week, at the end of twenty years, an investor could earn at least eighty thousand dollars. However, at the time this article was published, says Klingaman, Raskob was liquidating his stocks and getting out of the market. Klingaman also reveals the Federal Reserve Board's attempts to control speculation by increasing the rediscount rate on August 8, 1929, but points out that Americans were enjoying their prosperity and seemed to be swept up in the frenzy of stock speculation.

For a few brief shining moments, it looked as if everything would be all right.

There was no midsummer business slump in America in

29

1929. At the end of June, the high-quality glamour stocks—public utilities, railroads, and the industrial giants—resumed their rampage upward. With call money [money repayable on demand], hovering around the more reasonable level of 7 or 8 percent, Wall Street once more was filled with talk of a "roaring bull market" [in which prices are expected to rise]. On July 4, while the U.S. markets were closed for the holiday, American issues such as United States Steel, Pennsylvania Railroad, and the Atcheson, Topeka, and Santa Fe established record highs on the London Stock Exchange. By the middle of the month, the stock of the First National Bank of New York, "the aristocrat of all bank stocks," shot up $500 in a single day on the New York Curb Exchange, fetching a price of $7,900 per share. (George F. Baker, the bank's chairman, reportedly held twenty-two thousand shares of its stock, which meant that he had received a windfall profit of $11 million in the space of five hours.) U.S. Steel, which had retired its entire bonded debt by the simple expedient of issuing new shares of common stock, jumped nearly seven points on July 19, thereby adding another $51,152,184 to the value of its outstanding stock. Not to be outdone, AT&T eclipsed that mark by increasing its stock value by more than $75,800,000 in one day.

An Optimistic Outlook

As the good economic news continued to pour in, nobody worried very much about the Federal Reserve Board anymore. "This country is enjoying a surprising midsummer industrial boom, rarely equaled," crowed Arthur Brisbane, leading editorial writer for the Hearst chain of newspapers. Moody's Investor's Service confidently predicted that "as the year progresses, the probabilities are that much of the uncertainty will disappear and results for the full year make a very excellent showing." The steel industry continued to operate at nearly 95 percent capacity . . . newspapers carried reports of excellent corporate earnings for the first half of 1929—for companies ranging from Congress Cigar to White Rock Mineral Springs—which surpassed even the swollen profits of the comparable period in 1928 . . . industrial output for July showed a marked gain over 1928, though there was a slight and seemingly unimportant decline from the previous month . . . and the nation's investors received a record monthly sum of $863,355,828 in interest and dividend payments in July.

Much of that money was plowed right back into the stock market, as was a growing percentage of corporate profits. Although the bulls on Wall Street [who purchase stocks in a rising market, hoping to sell at a profit] were laughing at the impotence of the Federal Reserve Board in the summer of 1929, the fact was that the board had succeeded in pressuring its member banks to reduce their speculative loans. The slack had been taken up by corporations and wealthy, individuals; it was they, and not the banks, who were responsible for elevating the total of brokers' loans to the record-shattering sum of $5,813,000,000 in July. Standard Oil of New Jersey had an average of $69 million out on the call-money market every day. Warner Brothers, which had previously advised its employees that it would dismiss anyone caught playing the market, did an about face and formed its own bank to take advantage of the boom in security values, and a former vice-president of the National City Bank founded a new corporation—the First Call Money Company of America—specifically for the purpose of supplying speculative funds to the market.

Raskob's scheme . . . assumed that the stock market would continue to rise at its present rate, uninterrupted, for two entire decades.

The *New York Times'* index of fifty industrials rose fifty-two points in June, and then roared upward another twenty-five points in July. By no means, however, were these gains uniformly reflected across the board. A substantial portion of the issues traded on the New York Stock Exchange actually drifted downward throughout the summer, giving the list as a whole an exceptionally ragged appearance. At the time, few amateur investors paid any attention. . . .

Raskob's Scheme

Among the Empire State Building Corporation's board of directors were Pierre S. Du Pont and the project's guiding force, John J. Raskob. Raskob was spending the summer doing everything he could to perpetuate the illusion that stock prices could keep rising indefinitely. In May, he had revealed a scheme to introduce the installment buying plan to Wall Street; as Raskob explained it, he planned to form (sometime in the indefinite future) an investment trust company that would permit a factory mechanic in Detroit to purchase $500 worth of stock on margin by paying $200 down and negotiating a bank loan for the balance, putting up the stock as collateral and paying off the loan in installments of $25 per month. Raskob claimed that his motives were entirely altruistic—"I have all the money I want and now I want to help a lot of other people make some"—and he uttered soothing reassurances about the state of the stock market. "I have heard some opinions," he said, "that the present time is not opportune for investment because the general level of prices is too high and perhaps it's true that some stock may be selling at 20 per cent less in another year; but, in my judgment, many stocks are not too high even at their present level." Those who knew what Raskob was really doing behind the scenes probably laughed when they heard these reassuring words. When Raskob said that he already had "all the money" he wanted, what he meant was that he was quietly liquidating all his stock holdings and getting the hell out of the market. He certainly wasn't going to get caught in the storm when the bubble finally burst.

The board had waited too long to act, and its decision to increase interest rates succeeded only in introducing another element of uncertainty into an already wildly disarranged market situation.

His personal financial dealings in the summer of 1929 made Raskob's famous magazine article "Everybody Ought to Be Rich" a remarkable inside joke. Published in August in the *Ladies' Home Journal*, the article was based on Raskob's calculation that "if a man saves fifteen dollars a week and invests it in good common stocks, and allows the dividends and rights to accumulate, at the end of twenty years he will have at least eighty thousand dollars and an income from investments of around four hundred dollars a month. He will be rich. And because income can do that I am firm in my belief that anyone not only can be rich but ought to be rich." Of course, Raskob ignored the fact that the average weekly wage for American workers in 1929 was between $25 and $30, which meant that they could not save anywhere near $15 a week; moreover, Raskob's scheme obviously assumed that laymen could discern a sound stock from a dud (which most could not); and, most important, it assumed that the stock market would continue to rise at its present rate, uninterrupted, for two entire decades. . . .

Questioning the Federal Reserve Board

In Paris, Billy Durant [founder of General Motors and notorious stock market speculator], tenaciously continued his fight against the Federal Reserve Board and the bearish prophets of doom [those who believed the market would decline]. Striving mightily to maintain the mood of unrestrained optimism upon which the Hoover bull market depended, Durant fired another broadside at the board during a speech at the American Club at the end of May. "Say what you will," Durant insisted, "confidence—not half-way confidence, but 100 per cent confidence is the real basis for our prosperity. With all the wealth in the world, confidence lacking, we never could have reached the position we occupy today, and this great asset, confidence, should not be destroyed. That is the reason why the business men of America are almost a unit against the present policy of the Federal Reserve Board." Durant charged that the crashes in March and May, which he attributed directly to the perverse blundering of the board, already had led to the loss of hundreds of millions of dollars by "hundreds of thousands of people, who have contributed to the prosperity of America"; the result, he said, had been "fear, trembling and destruction of confidence, so essential to our prosperity." Upon his return to the United States at the end of June, Durant again assailed the Fed for "lining up with the destructive forces of Wall Street . . . fussing about brokers' loans, and interfering with business generally." "We can and will have a 'bull' market as soon as this question is settled," the Dream Maker predicted, "and when it is settled, seasoned securities of merit and those having possibilities will sell much higher than ever before.". . .

On Thursday, August 8, after the closing gong ended trading for the day on the New York Stock Exchange, the Federal Reserve Board announced that it was raising its rediscount rate from 5 to 6 percent. The news took Wall Street completely by surprise; after six months of indecision, no one expected the board to take such a bold step without warning. Apparently the action was precipitated by reports that brokers' loans had mounted to the staggering sum of $6,020,000,000, a perilous trend that could not be permitted to continue indefinitely without choking off credit to the rest of American industry. But once again the board had waited too long to act, and its decision to increase interest rates succeeded only in introducing another element of uncertainty into an already wildly disarranged market situation.

The following day, brokers began receiving "sell" orders well before the market opened at nine o'clock. As the *New York Times* reported, the Federal Reserve Board's announcement "put stockholders of the country into a frame of mind in which they wanted to get rid of their stocks to save such profits as existed, to prevent further losses or to 'get out of the market entirely,' as many did." As it turned out, they were the lucky ones.

The last three weeks of August represented the climax of America's long, exhilarating climb toward the evanescent pinnacle of prosperity.

Two billion dollars worth of stock values vanished in five stormy hours of panic-stricken selling. It was the heaviest day of trading since the precipitous decline of May 28; on the floor of the exchange, brokers angrily pushed and shoved one another to execute their stacks of sell orders. As measured by the *Times'* index, it was the most severe decline the market had suffered since 1911, when the newspaper began keeping track of such things. As usual, thinly margined accounts received the worst battering; hundreds of small speculators found themselves completely wiped out as their stocks plunged downward. "Any business that can't survive a one per cent raise must be skating on mighty thin ice," remarked Will Rogers acidly. (Rogers, incidentally, had taken [Bernard] Baruch's advice and reduced his own stock holdings to a minimum.) "Why, even the poor farmers took a raise of from six to ten per cent, with another ten per cent bonus, to get the loan from the banks," he added. "It took all that to completely break them, and nobody connected with the government paid any attention. But let Wall Street have a nightmare and the whole country has to help them get back in bed again."

Ocean liners installed brokerage branch offices, complete with short-wave radios and ship-to-shore telephones for their first-class passengers traveling to or from Europe.

Surveying the wreckage, Durant denounced the board's move as "only another blunder." "The day of reckoning is approaching," warned the man they called the King of the Bulls. "The business interests of this country are determined and will demand Congressional investigation and proper control of this group of men." Indeed, by virtually any measure the Federal Reserve Board appeared to have committed an egregious blunder. After the momentary panic of August 9, the speculative favorites on Wall Street recouped their losses almost at once and resumed an even more dizzying ascent, while the rest of the market kept inching downward in a slow, sad fall. The board's decision to raise its rates affected only its member banks, of course, and did nothing to restrain the ever-increasing flow of bootleg corporate loans to Wall Street; but it did put a further pinch on the farmers and small businessmen who had no other source of credit. One percentage point meant nothing to the speculators, but it threatened to push many legitimate businesses, already perched precariously on the edge, into failure and bankruptcy. "This will mean not only here, but all over the country, a tremendous curtailment of commercial, agricultural and real estate loans and cause great hardship and business depression," predicted former New Jersey governor Edward C. Stokes, then chairman of the board of First Mechanics National Bank. "This action will aid Wall Street's activities by drawing money to that centre through the highest rates offered to the loaner. It punishes . . . every security holder and legitimate borrower."

"The end of the story is not yet," warned the *New Republic:*

We may still see the pace of production and trade slackened on account of tight credit. If that happens, what will happen to the price of stocks, boosted far above any logical relation to their earnings even on the basis of present business activity? If the Federal Reserve authorities have no longer any power to moderate the overconfidence of the speculators, that may be after all the speculators' loss. We shall be lucky if many of the rest of us do not lose also.

For the rest of August the market presented a strikingly schizophrenic appearance. Stocks whose prices already far outstripped any rational measure of real value (some were now selling at thirty times annual earnings) kept rising ten, twenty, or even forty points per day—solely on the expectation that they could be passed on to someone else at a higher price in a day or two—while lower-priced stocks continued to decline. "It has been," observed the *New York Times* on August 22, "a confusing and perplexing performance."

A National Mania

The last three weeks of August represented the climax of America's long, exhilarating climb toward the evanescent pinnacle of prosperity. More than at any time since the bull market began five years earlier, the speculating public—at this point, slightly more than one million individuals carrying approximately three hundred million shares on margin—was blinded by the dazzling vision of a select group of stocks whose advance seemingly could not be checked by any force on earth. Even Owen Young got swept up in the madness in August, as he ventured back into the market to purchase nearly $2 million worth of stocks on margin. Brokerage firms in Manhattan reported a spectacular increase in business; the streets and subway stops around their uptown offices were thronged with customers, many of whom had given up their jobs as the value of their stock portfolios soared into hundreds of thousands of dollars. "By Stock Exchange opening time," observed John Brooks,

> all along Wall and Nassau, Broad and Broadway and Pine, the customers' rooms are jammed—there is standing room only and perhaps not even that, there is a premium on positions from which the quote board can be seen. Still, they all are sure it is worthwhile be-

ing there, right on the scene; they feel themselves to be part of something tremendous, and perhaps, too, they feel their physical presence in Wall Street makes them insiders, gives them some slight advantage over those who are maintaining the same vigil elsewhere—the barber or chauffeur or cab driver whose ear is cocked for a tip his important client may let fall, even the important man himself who has given up his vacation not in substance but only in spirit, and, sacrificing a seat in the sun, is glued all day to one in an office in Bar Harbor or Newport or Southampton or in a Catskill Mountain hotel.

Ocean liners installed brokerage branch offices, complete with short-wave radios and ship-to-shore telephones for their first-class passengers traveling to or from Europe. ("We were crowded in the cabin / Watching figures on the Board / It was midnight on the ocean / And a tempest loudly roared," went one parody.) At the U.S. amateur golf championship at Pebble Beach, California, E.F. Hutton and Company pitched a tent near the eighteenth green, where they set up a temporary office for the convenience of the gallery (and more than a few of the players, too). In the staid capitals of Europe, events on Wall Street dominated the minds and souls of the wealthy and fashionable set. "Scores of thousands of American shares are bought everyday in London alone," reported Viscount Rothermere sourly, "and Paris, Berlin, Brussels, and Amsterdam are pouring money into New York as fast as the cable can carry it. Wall Street has become a colossal suction-pump, which is draining the world of capital, and the suction is fast producing a vacuum over here."

"The Big Bull Market had become a national mania," recalled Frederick Lewis Allen. "Across the dinner table one heard fantastic stories of sudden fortunes: a young banker had put every dollar of his small capital into Niles-Bement-Pond and now was fixed for life; a widow had been able to buy a large country house with her winnings in Kennecott. Thousands speculated—and won, too—without the slightest knowledge of the nature of the company upon whose fortunes they were relying, like the people who bought Seaboard Air Line under the impression that it was an aviation stock." (It was really a railroad.) The *New York Times* carried a front-page story of a poor young Southern girl who had earned $4 working in the tobacco fields and tried to invest it in Standard Oil of New Jersey. In a letter to Standard Oil's offices, she explained innocently that she wanted to purchase "as little an intrest or shear in your Oil Wells as $4.00 to start with and then take what it makes for me and add to the four dollars until it amounts to a fifty dollar share for me." She asked the company to let her know when she could "start drawing money off of it." "I am a poor girl and I work on a farm with my home people," she said, "and I hired out to work in Tobacco to get this money which I want to put in the oil wells so I hope you will have a good heart and take this much to help me along a little and if you help me this much I hope the good Lord will bless you all in every way, so please answer real soon." Fortunately for her, the company sent the money back.

It is almost as if they believed the market existed for taking chances not on money but on happiness.

Some analysts believed that stock prices were being driven up primarily by the giant investment trusts, which had so much money at their command that they had to put it *somewhere*. And still people rushed to join every new trust that appeared; when the eminently reliable banking firm of Goldman, Sachs and Company formed the Blue Ridge Corporation investment trust with assets of $127.5 million in mid-August, shares sold at a premium, and the original issue was heavily oversubscribed within hours.

"Money is king," noted Brooks of those last frenzied weeks, "—but there is something else. It is a high, wild time, a time of riotous spirits and belief in magic rather than cold calculation, a time of Dionysius rather than Apollo. . . . It is almost as if they believed the market existed for taking chances not on money but on happiness."

"People sang louder, drank deeper, danced longer and squandered themselves in every direction," wrote playwright Ben Hecht. "They fornicated in cabanas, in rumble seats, under boardwalks. They built love nests like beavers and tripled their divorce rate. High, and many of the low, gave themselves hedonistically to the pleasures of the hour." The statistics supported Hecht's claim; America's divorce rate jumped to one out of every six marriages, the highest rate in the nation's history. . . .

Warning Signals

Like Jack Morgan [son of prominent financial adviser J. Pierpont Morgan], Bernard Baruch spent the better part of August rousting grouse on the moors of Scotland. Although he received a steady stream of optimistic reports from [Gerard] Swope and other friends at home extolling the strength of the American economy, Baruch hesitated to do anything more bold than purchase a few hundred shares of stock in a few obscure corporations he believed were undervalued. When he received an invitation to participate in Goldman, Sachs' new Blue Ridge investment trust (a company Baruch frankly described as "financial whoopee"), he requested advice from several trusted banking friends, including Charlie Mitchell [Chairman of the National City Bank], who were closer to the domestic scene. The first two replies were noncommittal, but on the sixteenth he received Mitchell's cabled response:

> GENERAL SITUATION LOOKS EXCEPTIONALLY SOUND
> WITH VERY FEW BAD SPOTS. . . . BELIEVE CREDIT SIT-
> UATION PRACTICALLY UNAFFECTED BY DISCOUNT
> RATE ACTION. MONEY SEASONABLY WEAK. SHOULD
> STRENGTHEN AS MONTH CLOSES. STRENGTH IN
> STOCK MARKET CENTERS LARGELY IN SPECIALTIES,
> WHICH IN MANY CASES SEEM UNDULY HIGH, WHILE
> THERE ARE MANY STOCKS, SUCH AS COPPER AND MO-
> TORS AND CERTAIN RAILS THAT LOOK UNJUSTIFIABLY
> LOW. I DOUBT IF ANYTHING THAT WILL NOT AFFECT
> BUSINESS CAN AFFECT THE MARKET, WHICH IS LIKE A
> WEATHER-VANE POINTING INTO A GALE OF PROSPER-
> ITY. BELIEVE THERE IS LESS PESSIMISM AROUND THAN
> WHEN YOU LEFT.

Yet Baruch was not so certain. "After I got this cable," he related some years later, "I went for a walk with General Pershing, who was my guest. We talked at length about the state of affairs in America, and I expressed my growing concern over the danger signs in the market. As we strolled along, I went over all the factors involved in the Shenandoah and Blue Ridge issues; even at a distance of three thou-

sand miles, I could see that these and many other enterprises were foolhardy. My intuition, which after all is only
the accumulated force of experience, was sending out warning signals." Baruch decided to cut short his vacation in
Scotland, and while he waited in London for his ship to de-
part for New York, Mitchell's exuberant message kept running through his mind. Several times Baruch cabled purchase instructions to his office in New York, only to
reconsider and countermand the orders each time. On the
voyage home, Baruch used the ship's brokerage wire to begin selling the stocks that remained in his portfolio. . . .

On August 10, Herbert Hoover celebrated his fifty-fifth
birthday at the presidential retreat on the Rapidan River in
Virginia. There were no more than a dozen guests, including journalists William Allen White and Mark Sullivan,
New York banker Jeremiah Milbank, and America's favorite
newlywed couple, Charles and Anne Lindbergh. Anne and
Herbert's wife, Lou, planned the birthday party, surprising
the President after he and his male guests had spent a busy
morning pitching horseshoes (Lindbergh won the title of
camp champ; Hoover just stood and watched), horseback
riding, and building a rock dam in a mountain stream—under the Great Engineer's direction—to form a sunning pool
for trout. After the party returned to the White House at
the close of the weekend (Lindbergh drove one car and
reached Washington far ahead of everyone else), Anne
wrote a letter to her mother, describing their visit: "We have
had really a lovely weekend—'slow' riding (suited to my
taste), walks down the stream, and around a fire at night.
For opinions I must wait. President and Mrs. Hoover have
been very kind. She is the most tireless, energetic hostess,
every moment given to thinking of and planning for her
large brood of guests. He has a nice dry wit."

But Hoover could not relax. He was oppressed with the
continuing problems of crime and farm relief and tariff reform. The Senate refused to give him discretionary power
to alter tariff rates because it feared he would set them too
low; in fact, the prohibitive import duties being discussed in
Congress already had brought a chorus of protest from
twenty-five foreign nations. When Hoover appeared at an
official welcoming ceremony at the fairgrounds in the
nearby town of Madison the following week, he seemed
pale and tired. "He spoke slowly," remarked one correspon-

dent, "and his appearance was that of a man who had not enjoyed a good night's rest," Some measure of Hoover's frustration with the unremitting rigors of life in Washington could be discerned in an uncharacteristically wistful and revealing speech to the gathering at the Madison fairgrounds. "I have discovered why Presidents take to fishing, the silent sport," he said:

> Apparently the only opportunity for refreshment of one's soul and clarification of one's thoughts by solitude to Presidents lies through fishing. . . . Fishing seems to be the sole avenue left to Presidents through which they may escape to their own thoughts and may live in their own imaginings and find relief from the pneumatic hammer of constant personal contacts, and refreshments of mind in the babble of rippling brooks. Moreover, it is a constant reminder of the democracy of life, of humility and of human frailty—for all men are equal before fishes. And it is desirable that the President of the United States should be periodically reminded of this fundamental fact, that the forces of nature discriminate for no man.

Such was the state of the President's mind on the eve of the Great Crash.

3

The Fruitless Efforts of the Federal Reserve Board

Frederick Lewis Allen

When stocks continued to rise at the close of 1928, the Federal Reserve Board increased the rediscount rate—the interest rate charged to banks that want to borrow money from the government—in hopes of making banks less willing to lend out money to speculators. The strategy didn't work. As the late historian Frederick Lewis Allen in the following excerpt from his 1931 work *Only Yesterday: An Informal History of the Nineteen-Twenties* notes, prices continued to rise into 1929 and speculators seemed to be willing to pay any amount to borrow money to participate in the booming market. According to Allen, the Federal Reserve Board needed a different strategy, and hoping to discourage speculation without deliberately initiating a crash, the Board asked Reserve Banks to refuse loans for speculative purposes. The immediate effect was a collapse in stock prices, but nonmember banks were still willing to offer loans to a public caught up in the speculative fever. The Federal Reserve Board was powerless to stop the frenzy. Allen studied at Harvard University and was an editor of the *Atlantic Monthly* and *Harper's Magazine*.

During that "Hoover bull market" of November, 1928, [in which stock market prices continued to rise], the records made earlier in the year were smashed to flinders. Had brokers once spoken with awe of the possibility of five-

Excerpt, as submitted, from *Only Yesterday: An Informal History of the Nineteen-Twenties* by Frederick Lewis Allen. Copyright 1931 by Frederick Lewis Allen. Copyright renewed 1959 by Agnes Rogers Allen. Reprinted by permission of HarperCollins Publishers, Inc.

42

million-share days? Five-million-share days were now occurring with monotonous regularity; on November 23rd
the volume of trading almost reached seven millions. Had
they been amazed at the rising prices of seats on the Stock
Exchange? In November a new mark of $580,000 was set.
Had they been disturbed that Radio [Corporation of Amer-
ica] should sell at such an exorbitant price as 150? Late in
November it was bringing 400. Ten-point gains and new
highs for all time were commonplace now. Montgomery
Ward, which the previous spring had been climbing toward
200, touched 439⅞ on November 30. The copper stocks
were skyrocketing; Packard climbed to 145; Wright Aero-
nautical flew as high as 263. Brokers' loans? Of course they
were higher than ever; but this, one was confidently told,
was merely a sign of prosperity—a sign that the American
people were buying on the part-payment plan a partnership
in the future progress of the country. Call money [repayable
on demand] rates? They ranged around 8 and 9 per cent; a
little high, perhaps, admitted the bulls, but what was the
harm if people chose to pay them? Business was not suffering from high money rates; business was doing better than
ever. The new era had arrived, and the abolition of poverty
was just around the corner.

Apparently speculators were ready to pay any
amount for money if only prices kept on
climbing.

In December the market broke again, and more sharply
than in June. There was one fearful day—Saturday, December 7th—when the weary ticker, dragging far behind the
trading on the floor, hammered out the story of a 72-point
decline in Radio. Horrified tape-watchers in the brokers'
offices saw the stock open at 361, struggle weakly up to 363,
and then take the bumps, point by point, all the way down
to 296—which at that moment seemed like a fire-sale figure. (The earnings of the Radio Corporation during the
first nine months of 1928 had been $7.54 per share, which
on the time-honored basis of "ten times earnings" would
have suggested the appropriateness of a price of not much
over 100; but the ten-times-earnings basis for prices had

long since been discarded. The market, as Max Winkler said, was discounting not only the future but the hereafter.) Montgomery Ward lost 29 points that same nerve-racking Saturday morning, and International Harvester slipped from 368½ to 307. But just as in June, the market righted itself at the moment when demoralization seemed to be setting in. A few uneasy weeks of ragged prices went by, and then the advance began once more.

The Federal Reserve authorities found themselves in an unhappy predicament. Speculation was clearly absorbing more and more of the surplus funds of the country. The inflation of credit was becoming more and more dangerous. The normal course for the Reserve banks at such a juncture would have been to raise the rediscount rate, thus forcing up the price of money for speculative purposes, rendering speculation less attractive, liquidating speculative loans, and reducing the volume of credit outstanding. But the Reserve banks had already raised the rate (in July) to 5 per cent, and speculation had been affected only momentarily. Apparently speculators were ready to pay any amount for money if only prices kept on climbing. The Reserve authorities had waited patiently for the speculative fever to cure itself and it had only become more violent. Things had now come to such a pass that if they raised the rate still further, they not only ran the risk of bringing about a terrific smash in the market—and of appearing to do so deliberately and wantonly—but also of seriously handicapping business by forcing it to pay a high rate for funds. Furthermore, they feared the further accumulation of gold in the United States and the effect which this might have upon world trade. And the Treasury had a final special concern about interest rates—it had its own financing to do, and Secretary Andrew Mellon was naturally not enthusiastic about forcing the Government to pay a fancy rate for money for its own current use. It almost seemed as if there were no way to deflation except through disaster.

A Different Course of Action

The Reserve Board finally met the dilemma by thinking up a new and ingenious scheme. They tried to prevent the reloaning of Reserve funds to brokers without raising the rediscount rate.

On February 2, 1929, they issued a statement in which

they said: "The Federal Reserve Act does not, in the opinion of the Federal Reserve Board, contemplate the use of the resources of the Federal Reserve Banks for the creation or extension of speculative credit. A member bank is not within its reasonable claims for rediscount facilities at its Federal Reserve Bank when it borrows either for the purpose of making speculative loans or for the purpose of maintaining speculative loans." A little less than a fortnight later the Board wrote to the various Reserve Banks asking them to "prevent as far as possible the diversion of Federal Reserve funds for the purpose of carrying loans based on securities." Meanwhile the Reserve Banks drastically reduced their holdings of securities purchased in the open market. But no increases in rediscount rates were permitted. Again and again, from February on, the directors of the New York Reserve Bank asked Washington for permission to lift the New York rate, and each time the permission was denied. The Board preferred to rely on their new policy.

The lesson was plain: the public simply would not be shaken out of the market by anything short of a major disaster.

The immediate result of the statement of February 2, 1929, was a brief overnight collapse in stock prices. The subsequent result, as the Reserve Banks proceeded to bring pressure on their member banks to borrow only for what were termed legitimate business purposes, was naturally a further increase in call-money rates. Late in March—after Herbert Hoover had entered the White House and the previous patron saint of prosperity, [Calvin Coolidge], had retired to Northampton to explore the delights of autobiography—the pinch in money came to a sudden and alarming climax. Stock prices had been falling for several days when on March 26th the rate for call money jumped from 12 per cent to 15, and then to 17, and finally to 20 per cent—the highest rate since the dismal days of 1921. Another dizzy drop in prices took place. The turnover in stocks on the Exchange broke the November record, reaching 8,246,740 shares. Once again thousands of requests for more margin found their way into speculators' mail-boxes, and thousands of participators in the future prosperity of the country were sold out with the loss of everything they owned. Once again the Big Bull Market appeared to be on its last legs.

Overriding Reserve Policy

That afternoon several of the New York banks decided to come to the rescue. Whatever they thought of the new policy of the Federal Reserve Board, they saw a possible panic brewing—and anything, they decided, was better than a panic. The next day Charles E. Mitchell, president of the National City Bank, announced that his bank was prepared to lend twenty million dollars on call, of which five million would be available at 15 per cent, five million more at 16 per cent, and so on up to 20 per cent. Mr. Mitchell's action—which was described by Senator Carter Glass as a slap in the face of the Reserve Board—served to peg the call money rate at 15 per cent and the threatened panic was averted.

Whereupon stocks not only ceased their precipitous fall, but cheerfully recovered!

The lesson was plain: the public simply would not be shaken out of the market by anything short of a major disaster.

During the next month or two stocks rose and fell uncertainly, sinking dismally for a time in May, and the level of brokers' loans dipped a little, but no general liquidation took place. Gradually money began to find its way more plentifully into speculative use despite the barriers raised by the Federal Reserve Board. A corporation could easily find plenty of ways to put its surplus cash out on call at 8 or 9 per cent without doing it through a member bank of the Federal Reserve System; corporations were eager to put their funds to such remunerative use, as the increase in loans "for others" showed; and the member banks themselves, realizing this, were showing signs of restiveness. When June came, the advance in prices began once more, almost as if nothing had happened. The Reserve authorities were beaten.

4

Women in the Stock Market: The Ladies of the Ticker

Eunice Fuller Barnard

A growing number of women began to participate in the booming stock market of the late 1920s. In the following article published in the April 1929 issue of the *North American Review*, a journal of literature and culture, Eunice Fuller Barnard reveals the type of woman who speculates in the stock market. She also provides reasons for their increased participation, and exposes the discrimination many women face in the market. For example, Barnard claims that women from a variety of backgrounds and income levels—from heiresses to washerwomen—participate in stock speculation. One reason for this increase, says Barnard, is that the women of the 1920s have their own money to invest. However, at the time Barnard wrote her article, no women yet held a seat on the exchange. In addition to writing for the *North American Review*, Barnard worked as a staff writer for *The New York Times*.

It might almost have been a club. The same discreet lighting, the cavernous davenports, an occasional bronze. In the deep Florentine armchairs a dozen women lounged and smoked.

But at one end of the room their gaze was transfixed by a wide-moving ribbon of light. "PAK—¾ . . . BDLA—½"— the cabalistic symbols glided across the magnified ticker tape. At the blackboard two blue-smocked girls, their

Reprinted from "Ladies of the Ticker," by Eunice Fuller Barnard in the *North American Review*, April 1929. Reprinted with permission.

leather belts bulging with cardboard checks, sprang nimbly about, changing the posted stock prices to correspond. And drowsily over all came the staccato drone of a half-dozen tickers, now blending, now breaking in on the subdued comments of the women.

"Almost noon!" yawned the domestic-looking young woman. "How the time does go in here! That RKK ought to start pretty soon. She generally runs toward the middle of the day."

"But look how Steel is breaking!" countered a firm, middle-aged voice. "That ought to mean something. A big market by the first of the week. I have a tip, but I always watch them awhile first. Now Copper I wouldn't—"

The nervous little gray-haired person in front dropped her "tip sheet". "Did you say Copper? she faltered.

On the other side the voice of the woman in the fur coat cut across. "Even if I have to sell short," she was protesting. "And I promised my husband I'd never do that."

The sprucely tailored woman manager, one eye on the ticker, passed by on her way to the telephone. One by one her young assistants, smartly turned out as so many mannequins, disappeared into the trading booth for a surreptitious sandwich, in lieu of luncheon. But the customers sat steadily on, lunchless, never missing a flicker of the tape.

The Growth of Women Investors

So Wall Street has come to Fifth Avenue. Silently one by one among the smart specialty shops of the Forties and Fifties appear the brokers' signs. With the arts of the drawing room, stock market operators for the first time in history are actually bidding for feminine favor. And woman is at last being made free of those more or less green pastures where men long have dallied.

For a year, indeed, all through the recent bull market [in which prices are expected to rise], women by the hundreds have sat, and even stood, in tense rows in the special stockbrokers' rooms set aside for them in various hotels of Upper Broadway. Day in and day out through a long five hours, aggressive, guttural dowagers, gum-chewing blondes, shrinking spinsters who look as if they belonged in a missionary-society meeting, watch, pencil in hand, from the opening of the market till the belated ticker drones its last in the middle of the afternoon.

Now they are packed into a stuffy, littered back room adjoining the men's, and again ranged in a tapestried parlor, with a miniature beauty salon attached, to raise the spirits in time of loss. Sometimes there are sympathetic young men managers in the latest double-breasted coats of Broadway; sometimes business-like women in charge, looking critically at the references of would-be buyers-on-margin.

Women by the hundreds have sat, and even stood, in tense rows in the special stockbrokers' rooms set aside for them in various hotels of Upper Broadway.

Five years ago the average brokerage house still frowned on the woman customer. Some even now do so officially. But they are King Canutes forbidding the rising tide.[1] Around them already is the surge of women investors— stenographers, heiresses, business women, housewives. The financial expert of a metropolitan newspaper recently estimated that in the last decade the woman non-professional speculator in stocks has grown "from less than a two per cent to a thirty-five per cent factor of the huge army that daily gambles in the stock market." Others, more conservative, put it at twenty per cent.

At the same time a brokerage house with offices throughout the eastern half of the country, in advertising for women customers, stated that already one out of five of its many thousands of clients was a woman. "In the past year," announced another firm, "the growth of the woman investor and the woman speculator has been amazing, and it is getting larger almost weekly." In a few instances women now own the majority of stock in large corporations. And there are even brokers who believe that women quite as much as men made the speculative stock market of 1927–29.

However that may be, certainly one of the outstanding social phenomena of that market when its history comes to be written will be the fact that in its course women for the first time in this country on a large scale financially became

---

1. King Canute, weary of the flattery of his court, tried to prove his imperfection by sitting on his throne before the sea, commanding the tide not to come in, which of course it did, getting them all wet.

people. They became a recognized, if minor, factor in the vast new trading capitalist class. For one enterprising Victoria Woodhull in the 'Seventies, and one Hetty Green in the 'Nineties,[2] marked as sports of nature, today there are hundreds of women investing their own funds and often playing the stock market with as bold a front as men.

Nor are they women of any one class or any one part of the country. Some of the most picturesque stones of the recent boom times are told of unexpected types. A woman farmer in the Middle West, for instance, recently telephoned her woman broker in New York to buy her a hundred shares of an automobile stock at a certain price. By quick action the broker secured them for her—the only shares that changed hands that day at so low a figure. By the next day they had gone up twenty points. The telephone call had cost the woman farmer six dollars, but had netted her almost two thousand overnight. To the same woman broker a scrub-woman in a well known club handed over $15,000 in cash which she had made on the stock market, for reinvestment. Indeed, in many instances waitresses and telephone girls, cooks and washerwomen who, so to speak, stood in with the boss, are said to have invested their mites on a wealthy employer's advice and cleaned up modest fortunes.

On the contrary there was the banker's wife in Indianapolis who made her profits by acting against his counsel. A year or so ago on her own initiative she bought some stock in a large mail-order house. When it had a phenomenal rise, her husband, her broker, and various friends in financial circles all advised her to sell. Instead, she coolly bought more at the new high price. Again the stock skyrocketed, and her ultimate profits totalled half a million. In much the way another woman of wealth a year and a half ago decided to what she could do with ten thousand dollars in Wall Street. She, however, got expert brokers' advice and acted on it. In all her transactions she bought on a large margin, and today has made her $10,000 into $115,000. Of the women who similarly gambled and lost the stories are somehow not so rife. Perhaps their heroines are the haggard figures one sometimes sees about the new women's broker-

2. Victoria Woodhull was a social reformer, newspaper publisher, and women's-rights advocate. Hetty Green, considered the greatest woman financier in the world, inherited a large fortune from her father and managed it so well that she left an estate valued at $100 million.

age rooms, day after day at the ticker, watching tensely to recoup their losses.

Creating an Interest in the Market

Women are of course only an especially spectacular section of the general march on Wall Street in the last year. They have been swept along by some of the same urges that have carried shopkeepers and day laborers, clerks and farm hands, from every nook and corner of the country suddenly into a market which has been 80 to 90 per cent speculative. But many brokers insist that a special cause—namely, the radio—has been largely responsible for advertising stock trading to the home woman and the farm woman who never before thought of Wall Street. The review of the market for the day and Wall Street closing prices come over the loud speaker in the leisure hours of her afternoon, after the dinner dishes are washed and before she has to go out into the kitchen again to get supper. She listens in just as she does to the health and the travel talks. And if one of her neighbors has taken a flier in some special stock, her interest becomes absorbed.

There are even brokers who believe that women quite as much as men made the speculative stock market of 1927–29.

Then take the tabloid newspapers with their circulation of millions. Most of them carry hints on the best stock "buys" of the day as regularly as they do recipes and patterns. The housewife reads for instance that "Wright Aero" is going up today just as she does that fresh fish is now on the market and that strawberries are cheaper. Even some of the conservative women's magazines now also carry general investment advice.

More and more the mystery is being taken out of the regular stock columns of the newspaper for the ordinary woman. She no longer flips them by like so much Sanskrit. She finds that they are prices, much the same and quite as intelligible as those of the department store advertisement.

Moreover, many of the stocks they list have names more familiar to her than to her husband. She better than he knows the relative crush of customers at the five-and-ten-cent stores, in the various chain grocery and drug stores whose stocks are offered on the market. She has often had first-hand experience with the different mail-order houses. She answers the doorbell when the agent of the gas or electric light company comes on a stock-selling quest, in the recent drives for consumer ownership. Indeed, to that is attributed the fact that she is rather apt to own public utility stock.

Even when she personally does not become a stock market customer, it is often her influence, according to many brokers, that induces her husband to buy the stock of this or that chain store or department store at which she trades. Very potent in the case of even the most sheltered woman are the various local urges. At the height of the Bank of Italy excitement last year, it is said, Italian women with shawls over their heads and strings of children by the hand calmly penetrated the holy of holies of the men customers' rooms at the brokerage offices to watch the ticker.

Money of Their Own

Another thing necessary to woman's participation in the market was of course money of her own to invest. And that, in these last expansive years, she has undoubtedly achieved as never before. Last year some 95,000 women as heads of families made income tax returns on $400,000,000. Others paid taxes on $1,500,000,000.

One woman broker, for example, who personally handles 300 accounts, has mainly business women as clients—buyers for department stores, small shop owners, advertising writers. Some of them are earning $15,000 a year, living on half, and investing the rest. Often they buy stock in the companies for which they work, or in others whose soundness they know from first-hand experience.

Then there is the growing army of women of inherited wealth—widows, and daughters—who of recent years seem to be given more and more discretion in the handling of their estates. And there are the wives who do not appear separately on the income tax returns, but who are sometimes, so far as investments go, the real disposers of the family savings. Frequently brokers will mention a writer or an artist whose wife attends to all financial matters from paying the bills to investing the surplus or negotiating the loans. More and more commonly, too, it is the wife of a busy professional man who volunteers to watch the stocks in which they are jointly interested.

Quite naturally, it seems, in this world of more and more intense specialization for men, investing, like buying, might slip into the woman's rôle. Today, it is estimated, 85 per cent of the spending in America is already in her hands. The disposition of income for present goods—for food, clothes, service, and often education, travel, and automobiles—is largely and unquestioningly hers. Why should she not, with her increasing leisure, learn to buy securities for the family's future, quite as well as fur coats and antique furniture?

But before that day could come, of course, women as a class would need far more experience than they have thus far had with stock exchange vagaries. Up to the recent break woman's entry into the market has been almost wholly over a bed of roses. She has yet to show that she can hibernate with the bears when the heyday of quick profits is over, as it already seems to be. She has pragmatically to learn the painful lesson that buying stocks may mean sudden and devastating loss, as well as gain. And if, after the holocaust, she has any money left, she has in many cases to discover for herself the gulf fixed between rational investing and stock gambling as it has been going on the last two years. After the introduction with veil and orange blossoms, in other words, can she compose herself to the dishwashing and the darning?

The floor of the exchange has been better protected against women members than that of Congress.

The suggestion, however, that woman become the family's investment manager, is a far cry from yesterday when a woman's inability even to draw a check was a standing joke. But it is no further probably than are Helen Wills, Gertrude Ederle[3] and Amelia Earhart from the fainting females of the reign of Victoria. Indeed, doubt is currently being cast even on a figure so strongly entrenched in the popular imagination as the widow victimized out of her husband's life insurance by the first wily promotor. An insurance company's in-

---

3. Tennis great Helen Wills Moody won eight Wimbledon singles titles in the 1920s and 1930s and 31 other major tennis titles. Gertrude Ederle was the first woman to swim the English Channel, breaking the men's record by two hours in 1926.

vestigation of some 750 death payments to widows, involving $9,500, 000, recently disclosed that only 1.3 per cent of the total had been lost in speculation or in any other way, up to six years afterward. More than half was invested and yielding income. And the rest was being used for the purchase of homes and businesses or for the education of children.

What is the essential difference between a woman and a man today as an investor? A dozen bank officials and brokers interviewed on this point saw potentially very little. "Women," said an officer of one of New York's largest banks, "have shown that with training they can be as good handlers of securities as men."

"There are some women's accounts that nothing would induce me to accept," volunteered a woman broker, "but so are there some men's. It is all a matter of individual temperament. There are some people so nervously constituted that they should never buy anything more speculative than bonds."

"I have yet to find," said another, "such things as 'women's bonds' or 'women's stocks'. In my experience with about equal numbers of men and women clients, I have found women's market sense and women's word as good as men's."

The main difference, all agreed, is that men as a whole still have far more money to invest, and more experience in investing it, than have women. The reason why some brokerage houses today hold out against women's accounts is, in the majority opinion, because they do not think women have enough money to risk on the market, and they do not want the responsibility and annoyance of small inexperienced investors. "Still," mused a woman broker, "I should hate to tempt any of them with a large certified check."

Discrimination Against Women

Apparently it is often true—whether from inexperience, from a more meticulous type of mind, or from lack of other occupation—that women ask more questions and are generally more bother as brokerage customers than are men. Before investing, especially, they are, so to speak, more completely from Missouri [known as the "Show Me" state]. They want to know all about a company, its prospects and its history, before putting their money into it. In the end, according to one broker, that is the best kind of client to have, for she proceeds more cautiously, is less liable to get caught, and if she does, cannot claim that she was not fully informed. So prevalent indeed is this pseudo-maternal attitude of women toward their stock investments that many successful managers of women's accounts make a practice of calling their customers frequently on the telephone to give them detailed reports. Of course the other type of woman, who flies ignorantly into the market to put her money on this or that popular stock, much as she would on a racehorse, is common. But there are more women, reared in the school of small-income economy, who cannot be induced to operate on a falling market or to take a loan, even when their investments or their own businesses would profit by it. Their besetting sins in finance seem to be timidity and limited view rather than reckless plunging.

Men and women work in offices, ride in the subway, go to the theatre and shops together. But apparently they do not yet buy stocks together.

Certain discriminations, it should be noted, still exist in New York Stock Exchange rules against women as sellers of stock. Technically stock in a married woman's name is not a good delivery. This is not an arbitrary distinction on the part of the Exchange, but a provision to protect investors in various States where the laws still do not recognize a married woman as party to a contract.

Thus far too, although there is no rule against them, the floor of the Exchange has been better protected against women members than that of Congress. A woman, however, could not just buy a seat. As in any club, she would have to be admitted by vote of the membership committee. And it seems doubtful whether either she or they yet desire her presence in the hurly burly.

Moreover, even the board rooms of the brokerage houses, sometimes at seemingly unnecessary extra expense, keep the men and women customers separate. Men and women work in offices, ride in the subway, go to the theatre and shops together. But apparently they do not yet buy stocks together. "Men," said a woman broker, "do not want us in their board rooms. And I am sure," she added, surveying her interior-decorated domain, "we do not want a lot of men smoking cheap cigars in here."

But, camouflage it as they may, women are at last taking a hand in man's most exciting capitalistic game. For the first time they have the interest, the self-assurance, and the entrance fee. If they become intelligent players, and if to any extent they should win financial power, they would probably in our economic society, as a matter of pragmatic fact, do more to raise the level of the common respect for women as a class than all the hard-fought suffrage campaigns.

Chapter 2

The Panic on Wall Street

1

October 24, 1929: Black Thursday

John Kenneth Galbraith

John Kenneth Galbraith is professor emeritus of economics at Harvard University and author of *The Great Crash: 1929*, considered by many scholars to be the definitive account of the events surrounding the stock market crash of 1929. In the following excerpt from *The Great Crash*, Galbraith reviews the events of Black Thursday, October 24, 1929, the first day of the panic of 1929. The author narrates the events from the first mad scramble to sell to the more optimistic closing hour. He describes the efforts of New York's leading bankers to quell the panic that morning and recounts attempts by financial leaders to restore confidence in the days that followed. Reactions to the panic varied, writes Galbraith: While some believed business remained sound and speculation would resume unimpeded, others considered the panic as punishment for the relentless pursuit of riches that encouraged stock speculations. Galbraith's other works include *The Affluent Society* (1958), *The Liberal Hour* (1960), *Made to Last* (1964), and *The New Industrial State* (1967).

Thursday, October 24, is the first of the days which history—such as it is on the subject—identifies with the panic of 1929. Measured by disorder, fright, and confusion, it deserves to be so regarded. That day 12,894,650 shares changed hands, many of them at prices which shattered the dreams and the hopes of those who had owned them. Of all the mysteries of the stock exchange there is none so impen-

Excerpt from *The Great Crash: 1929* by John Kenneth Galbraith. Copyright © 1954, 1955, 1961, 1972, 1979, 1988 by John Kenneth Galbraith. Reprinted by permission of Houghton Mifflin Company. All rights reserved.

etrable as why there should be a buyer for everyone who seeks to sell. October 24, 1929, showed that what is mysterious is not inevitable. Often there were no buyers, and only after wide vertical declines could anyone be induced to bid.

The panic did not last all day. It was a phenomenon of the morning hours. The market opening itself was unspectacular, and for a while prices were firm. Volume, however, was very large, and soon prices began to sag. Once again the ticker dropped behind. Prices fell farther and faster, and the ticker lagged more and more. By eleven o'clock the market had degenerated into a wild, mad scramble to sell. In the crowded boardrooms across the country the ticker told of a frightful collapse. But the selected quotations coming in over the bond ticker also showed that current values were far below the ancient history of the tape. The uncertainty led more and more people to try to sell. Others, no longer able to respond to margin calls [by the lending broker to restore the difference between the purchase price and a prearranged level], were sold out. By eleven-thirty the market had surrendered to blind, relentless fear. This, indeed, was panic.

By eleven o'clock the market had degenerated into a wild, mad scramble to sell.

Outside the Exchange in Broad Street a weird roar could be beard. A crowd gathered. Police Commissioner Grover Whalen became aware that something was happening and dispatched a special police detail to Wall Street to insure the peace. More people came and waited, though apparently no one knew for what. A workman appeared atop one of the high buildings to accomplish some repairs, and the multitude assumed he was a would-be suicide and waited impatiently for him to jump. Crowds also formed around the branch offices of brokerage firms throughout the city and, indeed, throughout the country. Word of what was happening, or what was thought to be happening, was passed out by those who were within sight of the board or the Trans-Lux [an electronic display]. An observer thought that people's expressions showed "not so much suffering as a sort of horrified incredulity."[1] Rumor after rumor swept Wall Street and these outlying wakes. Stocks were now selling for nothing. The Chicago and Buffalo Exchanges had closed. A suicide wave was in progress, and eleven well-known speculators had already killed themselves.

At twelve-thirty the officials of the New York Stock Exchange closed the visitors gallery on the wild scenes below. One of the visitors who had just departed was showing his remarkable ability to be on hand with history. He was the former Chancellor of the Exchequer, Mr. Winston Churchill. It was he who in 1925 returned Britain to the gold standard and the overvalued pound. Accordingly, he was responsible for the strain which sent Montagu Norman [governor of the Bank of England], to plead in New York for easier money, which caused credit to be eased at the fatal time, which, in this academy view, in turn caused the boom. Now Churchill, it could be imagined, was viewing his awful handiwork.

There is no record of anyone's having reproached him. Economics was never his strong point, so (and wisely) it seems most unlikely that he reproached himself.

The Bankers' Coup

In New York at least the panic was over by noon. At noon the organized support appeared.

At twelve o'clock reporters learned that a meeting was convening at 23 Wall Street at the offices of J.P. Morgan and Company. The word quickly passed as to who was there—Charles E. Mitchell, the Chairman of the Board of the National City Bank, Albert H. Wiggin, the Chairman of the Chase National Bank, William C. Potter, the President of the Guaranty Trust Company, Seward Prosser, the Chairman of the Bankers Trust Company, and the host, Thomas W. Lamont, the senior partner of Morgan's. According to legend, during the panic of 1907 the elder Morgan had brought to a halt the discussion of whether to save the tottering Trust Company of America by saying that the place to stop the panic was there. It was stopped. Now, twenty-two years later, that drama was being re-enacted. The elder Morgan was dead. His son was in Europe. But equally determined men were moving in. They were the nation's most powerful financiers. They had not yet been pilloried and maligned by New Dealers. The very news that they would act would release people from the fear to which they had surrendered.

It did. A decision was quickly reached to pool resources to support the market. The meeting broke up, and Thomas

Lamont met with reporters. His manner was described as serious, but his words were reassuring. In what Frederick Lewis Allen later called one of the most remarkable understatements of all time, he told the newspapermen, "There has been a little distress selling on the Stock Exchange." He added that this was "due to a technical condition of the market" rather than any fundamental cause, and told the newsmen that things were "susceptible to betterment." The bankers, he let it be known, had decided to better things.

Word had already reached the floor of the Exchange that the bankers were meeting, and the news ticker had spread the magic word afield. Prices firmed at once and started to rise. Then at one-thirty Richard Whitney appeared on the floor and went to the post where steel was traded. Whitney was perhaps the best-known figure on the floor. He was one of the group of men of good background and appropriate education who, in that time, were expected to manage the affairs of the Exchange. Currently he was vice-president of the Exchange, but in the absence of E.H.H. Simmons in Hawaii he was serving as acting president. What was much more important at the moment, he was known as floor trader for Morgan's and, indeed, his older brother was a Morgan partner.

The very news that [the bankers] would act would release people from the fear to which they had surrendered.

As he made his way through the teeming crowd, Whitney appeared debonair and self-confident—some later described his manner as jaunty. (His own firm dealt largely in bonds, so it is improbable that he had been much involved in the turmoil of the morning.) At the Steel post he bid 205 for 10,000 shares. This was the price of the last sale, and the current bids were several points lower. In an operation that was totally devoid of normal commercial reticence, he got 200 shares and then left the rest of the order with the specialist. He continued on his way, placing similar orders for fifteen or twenty other stocks.

This was it. The bankers, obviously, had moved in. The effect was electric. Fear vanished and gave way to concern lest the new advance be missed. Prices boomed upward.

The bankers had, indeed, brought off a notable coup. Prices as they fell that morning kept crossing a large volume of stop-loss orders—orders calling for sales whenever a specified price was reached. Brokers had placed many of these orders for their own protection on the securities of customers who had not responded to calls for additional margin. Each of these stop-loss orders tripped more securities into the market and drove prices down farther. Each spasm of liquidation thus insured that another would follow. It was this literal chain reaction which the bankers checked, and they checked it decisively.

Mixed Reactions

In the closing hour, selling orders continuing to come in from across the country turned the market soft once more. Still, in its own way, the recovery on Black Thursday was as remarkable as the selling that made it so black. The *Times* industrials were off only 12 points, or a little more than a third of the loss of the previous day. Steel, the stock that Whitney had singled out to start the recovery, had opened that morning at 205½, a point or two above the previous close. At the lowest it was down to 193½ for a 12-point loss. Then it recovered to close at 206 for a surprising net gain of 2 points for this day. Montgomery Ward, which had opened at 83 and gone to 50, came back to 74. General Electric was at one point 32 points below its opening price and then came back 25 points. On the Curb, Goldman Sachs Trading Corporation opened at 81, dropped to 65, and then came back to 80. J.I. Case, maintaining a reputation for eccentric behavior that had brought much risk capital into the threshing machine business, made a net gain of 7 points for the day. Many had good reason to be grateful to the financial leaders of Wall Street.

Not everyone could be grateful to be sure. Across the country people were only dimly aware of the improvement. By early afternoon, when the market started up, the ticker was hours behind. Although the spot quotations on the bond ticker showed the improvement, the ticker itself continued to grind out the most dismal of news. And the news on the ticker was what counted. To many, many watchers it meant that they had been sold out and that their dream—in fact, their brief reality—of opulence had gone glimmering, together with home, car, furs, jewelry, and reputation. That the market, after breaking them, had recovered was the most chilling of comfort.

The recovery on Black Thursday was as remarkable as the selling that made it so black.

It was eight and a half minutes past seven that night before the ticker finished recording the day's misfortunes. In the boardrooms speculators who had been sold out since morning sat silently watching the tape. The habit of months or years, however idle it had now become, could not be abandoned at once. Then, as the final trades were registered, sorrowfully or grimly, according to their nature, they made their way out into the gathering night.

In Wall Street itself lights blazed from every office as clerks struggled to come abreast of the day's business. Messengers and boardroom boys, caught up in the excitement and untroubled by losses, went skylarking through the streets until the police arrived to quell them. Representatives of thirty-five of the largest wire houses assembled at the offices of Hornblower and Weeks and told the press on departing that the market was "fundamentally sound" and "technically in better condition than it has been in months." It was the unanimous view of those present that the worst had passed. The host firm dispatched a market letter which stated that "commencing with today's trading the market should start laying the foundation for the constructive advance which we believe will characterize 1930." Charles E. Mitchell announced that the trouble was "purely technical" and that "fundamentals remained unimpaired." Senator Carter Glass said the trouble was due largely to Charles E. Mitchell. Senator Wilson of Indiana attributed the crash to Democratic resistance to a higher tariff.

Restoring Confidence

On Friday and Saturday trading continued heavy—just under six million on Friday and over two million at the short session on Saturday. Prices, on the whole, were steady—the averages were a trifle up on Friday but slid off on Saturday. It was thought that the bankers were able to dispose of most of the securities they had acquired while shoring up the market on Thursday. Not only were things better, but everyone was clear as to who had made them so. The bankers had shown both their courage and their power, and the people applauded warmly and generously. The financial community, the *Times* said, now felt "secure in the knowledge that the most powerful banks in the country stood ready to prevent a recurrence [of panic]." As a result it had "relaxed its anxiety."

Perhaps never before or since have so many people taken the measure of economic prospects and found them so favorable as in the two days following the Thursday disaster. The optimism even included a note of self-congratulation. Colonel Ayres in Cleveland thought that no other country could have come through such a bad crash so well. Others pointed out that the prospects for business were good and that the stock market debacle would not make them any less favorable. No one knew, but it cannot be stressed too frequently, that for effective incantation knowledge is neither necessary nor assumed.

Perhaps never before or since have so many people taken the measure of economic prospects and found them so favorable as in the two days following the Thursday disaster.

Eugene M. Stevens, the President of the Continental Illinois Bank, said, "There is nothing in the business situation to justify any nervousness." Walter Teagle said there had been no "fundamental change" in the oil business to justify concern; Charles M. Schwab said that the steel business had been making "fundamental progress" toward stability and added that this "fundamentally sound condition" was responsible for the prosperity of the industry; Samuel Vauclain, Chairman of the Baldwin Locomotive Works, declared that "fundamentals are sound"; President Hoover said that "the fundamental business of the country, that is production and distribution of commodities, is on a sound and prosperous basis." President Hoover was asked to say something more specific about the market—for example, that stocks were now cheap—but he refused.

Many others joined in. Howard C. Hopson, the head of

Associated Gas and Electric, omitted the standard reference to fundamentals and thought it was "undoubtedly beneficial to the business interests of the country to have the gambling type of speculator eliminated." (Mr. Hopson, himself a speculator, although more of the sure-thing type, was also eliminated in due course.) A Boston investment trust took space in *The Wall Street Journal* to say, "S-T-E-A-D-Y Everybody! Calm thinking is in order. Heed the words of America's greatest bankers." A single dissonant note, though great in portent, went unnoticed. Speaking in Poughkeepsie, Governor Franklin D. Roosevelt criticized the "fever of speculation."

On Sunday there were sermons suggesting that a certain measure of divine retribution had been visited on the Republic and that it had not been entirely unmerited. People had lost sight of spiritual values in their single-minded pursuit of riches. Now they had had their lesson.

Almost everyone believed that the heavenly knuckle-rapping was over and that speculation could be now resumed in earnest. The papers were full of the prospects for next week's market.

Stocks, it was agreed, were again cheap and accordingly there would be a heavy rush to buy. Numerous stories from the brokerage houses, some of them possibly inspired, told of a fabulous volume of buying orders which was piling up in anticipation of the opening of the market. In a concerted advertising campaign in Monday's papers, stock market firms urged the wisdom of picking up these bargains promptly. "We believe," said one house, "that the investor who purchases securities at this time with the discrimination that is always a condition of prudent investing, may do so with utmost confidence." On Monday the real disaster began.

Note

1. Edwin Lefèvre, "The Little Fellow in Wall Street," *The Saturday Evening Post*, January 4, 1930.

2

October 29, 1929: The Day the Bubble Burst

Gordon Thomas and Max Morgan-Witts

The final stock quote crossed the ticker at 5:32 P.M., on October 29, 1929, declaring over $16 million in total sales for a loss in share value of around $10 billion, twice the currency in circulation in the United States at the time. In the following excerpt from their book, *The Day the Bubble Burst: A Social History of the Wall Street Crash of 1929*, Gordon Thomas and Max Morgan-Witts narrate the experiences of some who witnessed the events surrounding the stock market crash, including William Crawford, the superintendent of the New York Stock Exchange, and Pat Bologna, speculator and owner of a shoeshine stand. The authors provide a vivid account of the pandemonium that erupted from the sound of the gong to the last quote of the ticker and walk the reader through the Exchange as stock prices fell in the mad rush to sell. According to the authors, the reactions were varied—from hysteria to tears—but most of the people involved in the stock market simply did not know what to do when the bubble finally burst on Wall Street that day. The authors have written many social histories of events including *The Day the World Ended, Earthquake: The Destruction of San Francisco*, and *Voyage of the Damned*.

Traveling into Wall Street, Pat Bologna [the owner of a shoeshine stand] was assailed on all sides by market talk. He was astonished to hear how good-natured were his fellow passengers. Bologna put it down to the surprisingly optimistic tone of the morning papers; apart from the

Times, most of the papers predicted that the situation would today be retrieved by "banking support." Bologna felt the subway train was "like the *Titanic*," with his fellow passengers putting on the same brave face as those on the great liner had reportedly done as she was sinking.

One of the subway passengers, a night manager in a Manhattan hotel, had a captive audience for his tale about a wealthy Midwest industrialist who had checked in the night before. The guest was a regular, with a standing order for a magnum of champagne and a call girl. As soon as he'd settled into his suite, the champagne was delivered—but the girl failed to materialize. The man rang the night manager, who promised to send a girl up. Moments later there was a knock on the suite door—and, when he opened it, the guest was confronted by a beautiful blonde. The impatient industrialist yanked her inside and told her to undress. The girl icily told him she was his broker's secretary. She handed the dumbfounded man a margin call for $400,000 and departed.[1] Minutes later, the desolate guest checked out, his sexual appetite, like his fortune, suddenly diminished.

Bologna was still chuckling over the story when he reached Wall Street.

An Uncertain Mood

There he found the mood pensive and somber. "People who had battled through Thursday's Crash, who had been hit again hard by Monday's break, looked like they couldn't take any more. They were at the end of their resistance."

Already the police, who had returned to patrol the district in large numbers, were directing the more obviously distressed to the Stock Exchange's medical department, a well-equipped office near the trading floor.

Normally, the department only treated Exchange members and their staff. After touring the district early this morning, its medical director, Dr. Francis Glazebrook, decided to open the facility to anyone who needed attention. Soon a number of cases of exhaustion and disorientation were being treated. The normally quiet medical department had become a busy frontline casualty station, its small team

---

1. When a security is purchased on margin, the buyer pays only a percentage of the purchase price and borrows the remainder from the broker, pledging the security as collateral. A fall in price reduces the margin available to the lender, who may ask the buyer to restore the margin.

of doctors and nurses prescribing sedatives and medicines before sending the more serious cases to one of the city hospitals for further treatment.

As the morning wore on, Dr. Glazebrook, a wiry, iron-gray man with the snap and precision of a military commander, realized he had potentially the busiest practice in Manhattan. The fifty-one-year-old doctor, who had treated shell-shock cases in the Great War, had seen enough in his tour of the district and the Exchange floor to recognize markedly similar symptoms in a number of people. He warned his staff they would probably become even busier when the market opened in an hour's time. . . .

The police, who had returned to patrol the district in large numbers, were directing the more obviously distressed to the Stock Exchange's medical department.

On the floor of the New York Stock Exchange, the mood around Post Twelve, Mike Meehan's Radio [Corporation of America] Post, had changed dramatically since the arrival of the gifted, mercurial Irishman and his team.

He had dressed in his "lucky" blue suit; a pearl pin held his tie in place. His shoes were burnished. He looked "like several million dollars—or a man going to a funeral."

Meehan's staff were equally smartly turned out. Heads had turned as they crossed the floor in a phalanx to their horseshoe-shaped trading enclave.

Incredibly, "the Irish Contingent"—the affectionate phrase used for the Radio specialist and his team—had never looked more relaxed or confident. They reminded one broker of "men about to lead the light brigade into that valley, and come out unscathed." Another felt, "if the Exchange ever struck a medal for coolness under fire, then Mike and his boys deserved one apiece."

Radio had taken a nose-dive. During yesterday it had been battered down nearly $19, crashing to a close of just $40.25 a share.

Overnight, thousands of sell orders for the stock had come in. Those who had bought Radio at the peak of $114.75 had subsequently watched their holdings fritter downward until yesterday's collapse. Now they wanted, or were forced, to get out before the stock fell still further. . . .

To maintain his appearance of almost total unconcern, Meehan left Post Twelve to tour the floor.

When he returned, he was still smiling. But Ed Schnell fancied he detected a change in his employer. He did not have to think hard for the reason. Schnell knew that Meehan had invested millions in the market, that Meehan's fortune, the security of his wife and children, even to some extent the future of his firm, were tied to the stocks he held.

Schnell did not know the extent of Meehan's personal loss so far, but even a brief tour of the trading floor was enough for his employer to learn his shares were more at risk than ever.

Yet, "typically, Mike didn't dwell on his own private problems. He just put everything he had into looking after Radio."

Now, as William Crawford, [Superintendent of the Stock Exchange], climbed the podium, Ed Schnell and his colleagues inside their stockadelike booth knew what it "must have been like for the defenders of the Alamo as they waited to be overrun."

Crawford's eyes swept the Exchange. Instinctively, he glanced toward the visitor's gallery. It was empty; it had not been reopened since its closure midday on Thursday. The superintendent was relieved reporters were unable to peer down on the bedlam already developing on the floor. Veteran traders, clerks, and page boys were running wildly around the perimeter before darting into the jostling mass in the center. The floor was littered with discarded pieces of paper.

The Market Opens

And, even as Crawford raised his gavel, the din from below increased to a "baying roar." The sound of the gong was lost.

"Twenty thousand at the market!"

"Thirty thousand—sell!"

"Fifty thousand! Sell at the market!"

General Oliver Bridgeman, U.S. Steel's battle-scarred specialist, flinched at the hammer blows. Steel plunged through yesterday's ruinous close of $186 a share with girderlike force.

The rest of the market tumbled with it, sucked swiftly

down by the uncontrollable crowd besieging Post Two.

During the first three minutes of trading 650,000 Steel shares were dumped on the market. At the end of those three minutes, few buyers were interested in the stock at $179. It seemed a lifetime since [Richard] Whitney had bid 205.

Steel's collapse created ugly panic. Men swore, shoved, and mauled, clawing at Bridgeman, forcing him to take refuge inside Post Two.

A messenger struggling through the crowd suddenly found himself yanked by his hair off his feet.

A messenger struggling through the crowd suddenly found himself yanked by his hair off his feet. The man who held him kept screaming he had been ruined. He would not let the boy go. The terrified youth at last broke free, leaving the man holding tufts of his hair. Crying in pain, the messenger fled the Exchange. His hair never regrew.

Behind, he left a scene of increasing pandemonium. As huge blocks of shares continued to be dumped at all seventeen trading posts, 1,000 brokers and a support army of 2,000 page boys, clerks, telephonists, operators of pneumatic message tubes, and official recorders could sense this was going to be the "day of the millionaire's slaughter."

William Crawford, swept along helplessly by the great tide of people, would always remember how "they roared like a lot of lions and tigers. They hollered and screamed, they clawed at one another's collars. It was like a bunch of crazy men."

By the time he found himself at Post Seven, in the center of the floor, the superintendent realized that something else was seriously wrong: The huge Translux screens, strategically placed around the vast hall, were blank. That meant the ticker was not running at all.

Crawford knew immediately what had happened. The panic selling had completely disrupted the flow of information about the buy and sell orders that traveled from the trading posts to the ticker staff.

Stunned, crushed in the crowd near Post Seven—where Air Reduction and Allied Chemical were leading the rout of stocks traded there—the superintendent was powerless to intervene.

Then, almost miraculously, the first share quotations began to judder across the screens; brokerage offices throughout the country were now receiving confirmation of the calamity occurring in New York.

A few feet away, at Post Twelve, Crawford could see Mike Meehan's mouth moving, but he could not hear what the broker was saying because of the noise.

Radio had fallen dizzily. In the first frantic moments of trading, its value had depreciated $10.25 a share. The stock was selling now for $30.

At the far end of the hall, at Post Seventeen, men were literally charging into the crowd in an effort to get to the specialist in International Telephone and Telegraph, whose stock had fallen $17 and showed no sign of stopping.

Suddenly a broker pitched to the floor and began to scramble about wildly. Before he was trampled underfoot he was dragged to the side. A nurse rushed to his aid; "the man was spluttering incoherencies." Convinced he was deranged, she sent for Dr. Glazebrook; he could commit the broker to Bellevue, the nearest mental hospital.

The medical director stooped beside his gibbering patient, pressing his ear close to the man's mouth. Then the doctor rose and smiled grimly; he told the nurse the man wasn't mad. He was incoherent because he had lost his false teeth while shouting an order. He had simply dropped to the floor in a vain attempt to find his dentures.

At Post Twelve—Ed Schnell's Alamo—the defenses were breached as sell orders for Radio poured in to the post. It seemed to Schnell, "the heavens had opened up, the stock was being pounded, down, down, right down to 26."

The young clerk marveled at the way Meehan conducted himself—accepting, never challenging anyone as the avalanche of orders spelled the demise of one of the most popular stocks of the Great Bull Market. . . .

The Madhouse

Dotted around the trading floor were some forty governors of the Stock Exchange. On heavy selling days in the past, it was said they had sometimes joined forces to create the basis for a rally by using the tens of millions of dollars they controlled to force some stability into the situation.

In today's selling maelstrom they were flotsam; out of touch with each other, separated by groups of near-demented men, the governors could do nothing to stem the ferocious waves of liquidation.

Richard Whitney was also on the floor. Pushed and shoved, like everyone else, the acting president was being almost totally ignored.

Out of touch with each other, separated by groups of near-demented men, the governors could do nothing to stem the ferocious waves of liquidation.

His appearance had at first raised the hope he had arrived to again make the saving gesture by bidding for a big block of U.S. Steel. But Whitney made no such move, and it was assumed the bankers' consortium had been disbanded. It had not, but the injection of funds it fed into the market for the purchase of shares was insufficient to make any noticeable difference. Whitney could only stand to the side and watch as the institution for which he was temporarily responsible transformed itself into a madhouse.

Superintendent Crawford eased himself down to the vicinity of Post Sixteen. There, Warner Bros' zigzag downward was being overhauled by the plunge in Safeway Stores and Simmons—the mattress company stock which had taken Winston Churchill's fancy.

A man, a complete stranger to Crawford, broke out of the crowd and lunged at another stranger—who sidestepped. The man careened on out of the main entrance into Wall Street, "screaming like a lunatic."

Shaken, feeling he was in the presence of "hunted things"—a phrase Whitney would also use later—William Crawford backed toward the staircase leading down to the basement.

He looked at his watch.

It was barely ten-thirty.

In all, 3,259,800 shares had been sold for a combined loss of over $2 billion in just thirty minutes. . . .

Pat Bologna waited anxiously for an answer over the pay telephone he was using close to his shoeshine stand. Unable to force his way into the nearby customers' room, he had requested by phone that the shares he held in National City be sold. He could not afford to put up the margin to keep them.

A clerk came on the line. Bologna's stock had been sold. Of the $5,000 the shoeblack had invested, he would get back $1,700. . . .

No Signs of Stopping

The panic carried uninterrupted into the early afternoon.

Steel was sinking toward $170. General Bridgeman and his staff were ankle-deep in paper.

At Post Five, eighty-six-year-old William Wadsworth—who had endured the 1907 panic and even earlier ones in the previous century—had never experienced such sustained fury. Men who normally treated the oldest broker on the floor with the deference his age and service demanded now hurled abuse at Wadsworth as they dumped rail stocks "by the bucketful."

Nearly all of the 751 investment trusts had been virtually wiped out; the trusts had been founded, one bitter critic was to write, "on the same solid economic principles as the promotions of the Middle Ages financing the alchemists attempting to transmute base metal into gold. They were designed mainly to attract the spare dollars poor people had saved."

Most of those savings had now vanished in the whirlwind of selling.

Steel, the rails, the coals, the motors were swept away with the stocks of corporations, oil companies, and the other giants of industry.

In all, 3,259,800 shares had been sold for a combined loss of over $2 billion in just thirty minutes.

Men wept openly in the Exchange. A few, doubtless for the first time in years, were driven to prayer, kneeling in impromptu supplication at the edge of the floor. Many went to nearby Trinity Church. It had totally filled for the thirty-minute service that began at noon, and would remain so for the rest of the day. For the first, and possibly only, time until now, Protestants, Catholics, and some Jews gathered together in Trinity, oblivious of its denomination, drawn there simply because it was a place of worship.

By early afternoon, Wall Street was blocked almost solid from Broadway to the river by an estimated ten thousand men and women. Rumors passed up and down the Street, bounced into adjoining streets, were enlarged, and bounced back into Wall.

Nobody knew what to believe; nobody knew how to behave.

There was no precedent for such a disaster.

By one o'clock, the orgy of selling on the Stock Exchange had risen to 12,652,000 shares.

It showed no sign of stopping. . . .

In New York the ticker kept running long after Crawford's closing gong at 3 P.M. Every falling share it recorded helped sound the death knell of the New Era.

America, the richest nation in the world, indeed the richest in all history—its 125 million people possessed more real wealth and real income, per person and in total, than the people of any other country—was now paying the price for accepting too many get-rich-quick schemes, the damaging duels fought between bulls and bears, pool operations and manipulations, buying on overly slim margins securities of low and even fraudulent quality. The indecisive and sometimes misleading leadership from the business and political world had contributed to the nationwide stampede to unload.

At 5:32 P.M. the final quotation clicked across the tickers of a numbed nation. The tape's operator signed off: TOTAL SALES TODAY 16,383,700. GOOD NIGHT.

Those millions of sales represented a loss in share value on the New York Exchange alone of some $10 billion. That was twice the amount of currency in circulation in the entire country at the time.

Eventually, the total lost in the financial pandemic would be put at a staggering $50 billion—all stemming from a virus that proved fatal on October 29, 1929: the day the bubble burst.

3

The Commercial Structure of the Nation Is Sound

Julius Klein

In a radio broadcast on the evening of the stock market crash, October 29, 1929, Assistant Secretary of Commerce, Dr. Julius Klein, addressed the nation, hoping to restore confidence and assure Americans that the New York Stock Exchange was not a barometer of business prosperity. According to Klein, only a small percentage of Americans actually participate in stock speculation, and those who suffered are victims of a boom psychology, in which naive speculators bought stocks hoping for quick profits with little knowledge of their actual dividend-paying capacity. The purchasing power of the majority of Americans who did not participate in speculation remains strong, Klein claims, and the industrial and commercial structure of the nation continues to be sound. The Secretary speaks of the decade's growth in income, the result of advances in technology and education. Although Klein says he cannot predict the nation's economic future, he is confident the nation's business leaders have the knowledge and experience to continue the advance of prosperity. Despite Klein's assurances, however, American confidence would soon be shaken as the nation slipped into the Great Depression.

O n Friday last the President [Herbert Hoover] stated that the fundamental business of the country, that is production and distribution of commodities, is on a sound

Radio speech given by Julius Klein, October 29, 1929.

and prosperous basis. The best evidence is that although production and consumption are at high levels, the average prices of commodities as a whole have not increased and there have been no appreciable increases in the stocks of manufactured goods.

However, there has been a tendency of wages to increase, and the output per worker in many industries again shows an increase, all of which indicates a healthy condition.

There is no reason today to change a single word of this statement of the President. Stock Exchange prices have gone down materially since Friday, but the stock market is not the major barometer of business, and a decline in security prices does not greatly affect the buying power of the community, on which buying power rents the activity of production, the earnings of corporations and other business enterprises and the employment of labor.

No one knows the number of persons engaged in this speculative activity, but even if we accepted the apparently liberal estimate of some non-official observers, who place the speculative accounts at about a million, these would still involve less than 4 per cent of all the families in the entire nation. Or, if we put it on the basis of individuals, the ratio would be less than 1 per cent of the total population.

Please don't misunderstand me or think that I am belittling the hardships of even this small fragment of our people, but even if all of these speculators suffered—and there were untold thousands who did not—you would still have a vastly preponderant majority of the nation unaffected by these speculative gyrations.

And remember, incidentally, to cite just one corrective of this situation, that these speculative accounts could be matched twice over by the more than 2,000,000 families who derive their livelihood from export trade, which is almost entirely unaffected by this movement.

The Problem of Speculation

Stock prices have gone down suddenly because over the past two or three years it seems to be generally agreed that they had risen much too rapidly. Throughout the past eight years, with very temporary and minor recessions, the production of goods and service in the United States has gradually but, on the whole, very considerably increased.

That is the same thing as saying that national income

increased. This naturally added to the profits of business, especially as, at the same time, many economies in production methods were introduced. The increased profits of business justified an advance in stock price but they did not justify going up to the sky.

It would have been proper, no doubt, for stocks to rise in price somewhat faster than actual production of commodities because of the gradual spread among the people of confidence in the general future of American business, of confidence that the increase of production in commodities and profits of industry would in the long run continue.

Over the past two or three years it seems to be generally agreed that [stock prices] had risen much too rapidly.

Such a conviction might justify some discounting of future larger earnings in the prices of securities. It did not justify carrying them to such a level that in many cases only hope for corporate earnings that would pay a fair rate of return on the prices paid for stocks.

We have been under the influence, as regards stock prices, of a boom psychology. Many persons have bought stocks with little knowledge of their present or probable future dividend-paying capacity. Many, moreover, have borrowed money in order to make these stock purchases.

A reaction was bound to occur. The main point which I want to emphasize is the fundamental soundness of that great mass of economic activities on which the well-being of the vast majority of us all depends. One may have due sympathy for the very considerable number who have lost money in the stock market without losing sight of the fact that there has been no change in the situation of the overwhelming majority of American families. The growth of the income of the nation and the advance in the well-being of its businessmen, its wage earners and its farmers during recent years has not been due to boom psychology nor to temporary and fleeting causes.

It has been a definite upward trend, not a wave, whose subsidence would leave us in a deep trough.

The fundamental cause of the expansion of business and

the improvement in standards of living has been the growing efficiency of production. We have been able to produce more and more goods and services per person at work. This gain in efficiency in turn has been due to causes of an enduring and cumulative character, causes that enter into the very bodies and minds of our people and into the very foundations of our economic structure.

The steady spread of education is perhaps the most basic of those upward-pushing forces. Closely allied with this is the growth of scientific research with its harvest of inventions and discoveries. The abundant savings of the people, with the consequent expansion of our capital have enabled us to provide more and better equipment for production, thus reducing costs. One could readily name other basic factors which have contributed to our progress and which are just as real and powerful today as they were a month ago and far more powerful than they were even eight or ten years ago.

A Steady Economy

The most conclusive evidence that the progress of American industry and commerce in recent years has not been fictitious, has not been a mere inflationary boom, lies in the steadiness of prices of commodities. Against the immense advance in prices of securities, those of goods and services have for years been stationary or with a slight downward trend. A business boom which threatens a subsequent collapse of business is always accompanied by considerable, if not great, advance in commodity prices.

Some of you may be expecting me to tell you what is going to happen to stock prices tomorrow and next week. If you pause to think about it, however, you will realize that it would be quite improper as well as impossible for any government official to give out such an opinion. The careful student of American economic life, equipped with an abundance of statistics, can forecast fairly well the long-time trends of production and of standards of living and even of many more specific branches of business or other economic aspects. He cannot foresee accurately short-time changes in economic conditions and least of all those speculative changes which depend largely upon the psychology of the people or a fraction of the people. All of us are justified, in my opinion, in a profound confidence in the general economic future of the country. Just what relation should exist between that confidence and his present attitude toward the stock market is something for each individual to decide for himself.

Broadly speaking, our average per capita production has increased by from 50 to 75 per cent since 1900 and by from 25 to 35 per cent since 1919, and remember that 1919 was not a depression year but one of high activity. I fully believe that the causes which have brought about this great advance will accomplish as much during the next decade or the next quarter of a century. There may be temporary recessions but these can be reduced to a minimum if we all have confidence in the general upward trend. Many of the business depressions of past decades have been primarily psychological and could have been avoided or minimized if the businessmen and the masses of the people had had the proper confidence in themselves. The general public of today understands better than ever before the long term trends of our economic life and the fundamental forces at work in it. I believe that we have very good reason to anticipate that this great knowledge will breed greater confidence and will prevent us from giving way in any large measure to a defeatist psychology. . . .

The factors have not been changed by the drop in stock prices. The national income of the United Sates at this moment is hardly a fraction less than it was a month ago. Established indexes, such as the quantity of output of our farms, our mines and our factories, and the volume of our railroad transportation, support this view.

Our commercial and industrial corporations are headed by men of broad vision, high qualifications and large experience with the intricate problems of our complex economic scheme.

The number of citizens whose buying ability has been affected by the decline in the value of speculative securities is not very large. Their purchases do not make up a very significant fraction of the demand for goods. There is no reason why the twenty-five or more million families, representing over 95 per cent of our population, whose incomes remain undiminished, should cut down their purchases of commodities, and therefore, very few industrials should see any appreciable reduction in the sales of their output. Aside from purchase of goods by consumers for their own actual use, the biggest demand for commodities is that for expanding what the economists call the capital equipment of the nation.

In normal times there is an immense call for building materials, steel, machinery, railroad equipment, and many other classes of goods for the purpose of building and equipping factories, public works and other productive enterprises. At least a tenth and perhaps an eighth of the productive energy is normally devoted to this creation of capital goods. If our businessmen and our people maintain that confidence in the future which the long experience of the past fully justifies, we shall see no diminution in the demand for capital goods as the result of the break in stock prices. On the contrary, the diversion of capital from stock market speculation to direct productive enterprise might readily increase the demand for commodities of this sort.

Ground for Confidence

One of the major grounds for confidence in the steadiness of American industry lies in the widespread dissemination of better statistical information and the practice of businessmen in guiding their policies in the light of such statistics. Never before has American industry and commerce been so ably managed as at present. Our commercial and industrial corporations are headed by men of broad vision, high qualifications and large experience with the intricate problems of our complex economic scheme. More than this, the executives of American business have today at their finger tips current facts upon the movement of their own industries, allied industries and all industry and business which in the last analysis, because of the interdependence between industry and industry, is of great importance. Rule of thumb practices have long since given way to policies based upon proper facts and analysis.

The businessman who is momentarily disturbed by the sharp decline in stock prices will glance at the current statistics of other economic factors. He will find, for example, that in September—of course, actual October figures are not yet available—industrial employment was 5 per cent greater than a year ago, and that the amount of wage payments by our factories was 8 per cent larger than in September last year. He will see no ground for expecting reduced purchases of commodities on the part of the wage-earner. He will find that there has been no accumulation of stocks of manufactured goods because of over-anticipation of future demand or because of any present falling off in demand. The American Railway Association, which collects advice "as to the probable demands for cars," has received reports indicating freight car requirements for the present quarter are more than 2 per cent greater than for the same quarter of 1928. This demand for freight cars reflects the production of and demand for goods.

Regardless of regrettable speculative uncertainty, the industrial and commercial structure of the nation is sound.

Again, the statistics show the farmer in a relatively favorable condition and his demand for manufactured goods may well be expected to remain strong. The quantity of crop production this year has been almost as great as last year, when the income of the farmer was the highest in history. One cannot, of course, forecast the price of farm products but thus far they are practically the same as a year ago.

We must not forget, moreover, that export trade has become a very important factor in American business. Exports of manufactured goods especially have increased steadily and rapidly in recent years. We now export approximately 10 per cent of the total output of our factories. There is no reason to anticipate any decline in this big factor in demand and on the contrary the upward movement of recent years is likely to continue.

One of the major indications of general prosperity is the amount of new life insurance taken out. Sales of insurance were 15 per cent greater last month than in September, 1928, and every recent year has shown a gain in the annual volume of new insurance, until today we have the truly prodigious total of over 100 billions of insurance now in force. Some small fragment of this doubtless was bought with the proceeds of speculation, but by far the greater part stands as a mighty symbol of the inherent economic soundness as well as the far-sighted frugality of our nation.

After all, the volume of our purchasing power measures the heights of living standards; it is the impressive manifestation of our highest wage rates. And, basically, our normal purchasing power has not been appreciably impaired. Regardless of regrettable speculative uncertainty, the industrial and commercial structure of the nation is sound.

4
Personal Recollections of Loss and Survival

Studs Terkel

In the following excerpts from *Hard Times: An Oral History of the Great Depression*, Studs Terkel, considered by many to be one of the greatest oral historians of the twentieth century, chronicles the recollections of several people who experienced firsthand the stock market crash of 1929. For example, Terkel interviews Arthur A. Robertson, an industrialist who sold most of his stocks in May of 1929, months before the October crash. Many of his friends, however, were not so lucky. Robertson recalls his relationship with Jesse Livermore, a notorious stock market speculator, who after substantial losses in the crash made a comeback with Robertson's help. Livermore continued to speculate, only to lose his fortune again, ultimately shooting himself in the bathroom of a New York restaurant. Terkel also interviews investment brokers who describe the confusion and despair and have developed their own conclusions about the causes of the crash. While some recall their financial struggles after the crash, others who were lucky enough to make a living during the depression, remember that most of those who suffered accepted responsibility for their fate.

Arthur A. Robertson

*H*is offices are on an upper floor of a New York skyscraper. On the walls are paintings and photographs. A portrait of President Johnson is inscribed "To my friend, a patriot who serves his country." Another, of Hubert Humphrey—"To my friend, Arthur Robertson, with all my good wishes." Also, a photograph of Dwight

Excerpted from *Hard Times: An Oral History of the Great Depression*, edited by Studs Terkel (New York: Pantheon). Copyright © 1970 by Studs Terkel. Reprinted with permission from Donadio & Olson as agents for the author.

Eisenhower: "To my friend, Arthur Robertson." There are other mementoes of appreciation from Americans in high places.

He recounts his early days as a war correspondent, advertising man and engineer. "We built a section of the Sixth Avenue subway. I've had a peculiar kind of career. I'm an industrialist. I had been in Germany where I picked up a number of porcelain enamel plants. I had a hog's hair concession from the Russian government. I used to sell them to the outdoor advertising plants for brushes. With several associates, I bought a company nineteen years ago for $1,600,000. We're on the New York Stock Exchange now and recently turned down $200 million for it. I'm chairman of the board, I control the company, I built it.

"I thought seriously of retiring in 1928 when I was thirty. I had seven figures by the time I was twenty-four."

In 1929, it was strictly a gambling casino with loaded dice. The few sharks taking advantage of the multitude of suckers. It was exchanging expensive dogs for expensive cats. There had been a recession in 1921. We came out of it about 1924. Then began the climb, the spurt, with no limit stakes. Frenzied finance that made Ponzi[1] look like an amateur. I saw shoeshine boys buying $50,000 worth of stock with $500 down. Everything was bought on hope.

I saw shoeshine boys buying $50,000 worth of stock with $500 down. Everything was bought on hope.

Today, if you want to buy $100 worth of stock, you have to put up $80 and the broker will put up $20. In those days, you could put up $8 or $10. That was really responsible for the collapse. The slightest shake-up caused calamity because people didn't have the money required to cover the other $90 or so. There were not the controls you have today. They just sold you out: an unwilling seller to an unwilling buyer.

A cigar stock at the time was selling for $115 a share. The market collapsed. I got a call from the company president. Could I loan him $200 million? I refused, because at the time I had to protect my own fences, including those of

1. A Boston financier of the Twenties. His "empire" crashed, many people were ruined. He went to prison.

my closest friends. His $115 stock dropped to $2 and he jumped out of the window of his Wall Street office.

There was a man who headed a company that had $17 million in cash. He was one of the leaders of his industry and controlled three or four situations that are today household words. When his stock began to drop, he began to protect it. When he came out of the second drop, the man was completely wiped out. He owed three banks a million dollars each.

It was very dark. You saw people who yesterday rode around in Cadillacs lucky now to have carfare.

The banks were in the same position he was, except that the government came to their aid and saved them. Suddenly they became holier than thou, and took over the businesses of the companies that owed them money. They discharged the experts, who had built the businesses, and put in their own men. I bought one of these companies from the banks. They sold it to me in order to stop their losses.

The worst day-to-day operators of businesses are bankers. They are great when it comes to scrutinizing a balance sheet. By training they're conservative, because they're loaning you other people's money. Consequently, they do not take the calculated risks operating businesses requires. They were losing so much money that they were tickled to get it off their backs. I recently sold it for $2 million. I bought it in 1933 for $33,000.

In the early Thirties, I was known as a scavenger. I used to buy broken-down businesses that banks took over. That was one of my best eras of prosperity. The whole period was characterized by men who were legends. When you talked about $1 million you were talking about loose change. Three or four of these men would get together, run up a stock to ridiculous prices and unload it on the unsuspecting public. The minute you heard of a man like [Billy] Durant or Jesse Livermore buying stock, everybody followed. They knew it was going to go up. The only problem was to get out before they dumped it.

Durant owned General Motors twice and lost it twice

. . . was worth way in excess of a billion dollars on paper, by present standards, four or five billion. He started his own automobile company, and it went under. When the Crash came, he caved in, like the rest of 'em. The last I heard of him I was told he ended up running a bowling alley. It was all on paper. Everybody in those days expected the sun to shine forever.

October 29, 1929, yeah. A frenzy. I must have gotten calls from a dozen and a half friends who were desperate. In each case, there was no sense in loaning them the money that they would give the broker. Tomorrow they'd be worse off than yesterday. Suicides, left and right, made a terrific impression on me, of course. People I knew. It was heartbreaking. One day you saw the prices at a hundred, the next day at $20, at $15.

On Wall Street, the people walked around like zombies. It was like *Death Takes A Holiday.* It was very dark. You saw people who yesterday rode around in Cadillacs lucky now to have carfare.

One of my friends said to me, "If things keep on as they are, we'll all have to go begging." I asked, "Who from?"

Many brokers did not lose money. They made fortunes on commissions while their customers went broke. The only brokers that got hurt badly were those that gambled on their own—or failed to sell out in time customers' accounts that were underwater. Of course, the brokerage business fell off badly, and practically all pulled in their belts, closed down offices and threw people out of work.

Banks used to get eighteen percent for call money— money with which to buy stock that paid perhaps one or two-percent dividends. They figured the price would continue to rise. Everybody was banking on it. I used to receive as much as twenty-two percent from brokers who borrowed from me. Twenty-two percent for money!

The Great Speculators

Men who built empires in utilities, would buy a small utility, add a big profit to it for themselves and sell it back to their own public company. That's how some like Samuel Insull became immensely wealthy. The thing that caused the Insull crash is the same that caused all these frenzied financiers to go broke. No matter how much they had, they'd pyramid it for more.

I had a great friend, John Hertz. At one time he owned ninety percent of the Yellow Cab stock. John also owned the Checker Cab. He also owned the Surface Line buses of Chicago. He was reputed to be worth $400 to $500 million. He asked me one day to join him on a yacht. There I met two men of such stature that I was in awe: Durant and Jesse Livermore.

We talked of all their holdings. Livermore said: "I own what I believe to be the controlling stock of IBM and Philip Morris." So I asked, "Why do you bother with anything else?" He answered, "I only understand stock. I can't bother with businesses." So I asked, "Do men of your kind put away $10 million where nobody can ever touch it?" He looked at me and answered, "Young man, what's the use of having ten million if you can't have big money?"

When I left my house, I checked with my broker. By the time I reached my office, I had made sixty-five points.

In 1934—after he went through two bankruptcies in succession—my accountant asked if I'd back Livermore. He was broke and wanted to make a comeback in the market. He always made a comeback and paid everybody off with interest. I agreed to do it. I put up $400,000. By 1939, we made enough money so that each of us could have $1,300,000 profit after taxes. Jesse was by this time in his late sixties, having gone through two bankruptcies. "Wouldn't it be wise to cash in?" I asked him. In those days, you could live like a king for $50,000 a year. He said he could just never get along on a pittance.

So I sold out, took my profits, and left Jesse on his own. He kept telling me he was going to make the killing of the century. Ben Smith, known as "Sell 'Em Short Ben," was in Europe and told him there was not going to be a war. Believing in Smith, Livermore went short on grain.[2] For every

---

2. "Selling short is selling something you don't have and buying it back in order to cover it. You think a stock is not worth what it's selling for, say its listed as $100. You sell a hundred shares of it, though you haven't got the stock. If you are right, and it goes down to $85, you buy it at that price, and deliver it to the fellow to whom you sold it for $100. You sell what you don't have." Obviously, if the stock rises in value, selling short is ruinous. . . . Ben Smith sold short during the Crash and made "a fortune."

dollar he owned, plus everything he could pyramid.

When I arrived in Argentina, I learned that Germany invaded Poland. Poor Jesse was on the phone. "Art, you have to save me." I refused to do anything, being so far away. I knew it would be throwing good money after bad.

Our investment company went up to two, three hundred, and then went down to practically nothing. As all investment companies did.

A couple of months later, I was back in New York, with Jesse waiting for me in my office. The poor fellow had lost everything he could lay his hands on. He asked for a $5,000 loan, which, of course, I gave him. Three days later, Jesse had gone to eat breakfast in the Sherry-Netherlands, went to the lavatory and shot himself. They found a note made out to me for $5,000. This was the man who said, "What's the use having ten million if you can't have big money?" Jesse was one of the most brilliant minds in the trading world. He knew the crops of every area where grain grew. He was a great student, but always over-optimistic.

Did you sense the Crash coming in 1929?

I recognized it in May and saved myself a lot of money. I sold a good deal of my stocks in May. It was a case of becoming frightened. But, of course, I did not sell out completely, and finished with a very substantial loss.

In 1927 when I read [Charles] Lindbergh was planning his memorable flight, I bought Wright Aeronautic stock. He was going to fly in a plane I heard was made by Wright. I lived in Milwaukee then. My office was about a mile from my home. When I left my house, I checked with my broker. By the time I reached my office, I had made sixty-five points. The idea of everything moving so fast was frightening. Everything you bought just seemed to have no ceiling.

People say we're getting a repetition of 1929. I don't see how it is possible. Today with Securities and Exchange Commission (SEC) controls and bank insurance, people know their savings are safe. If everybody believes, it's like believing in counterfeit money. Until it's caught, it serves its purpose.

In 1932 I came to New York to open an office in the Flatiron Building. Macfadden, the health faddist, created penny restaurants. There was a Negro chap I took a liking to that I had to deal with. He agreed to line up seventy-five people who needed to be fed. At six o'clock I would leave my office, I'd march seventy-five of 'em into the Macfadden restaurant and I'd feed 'em for seven cents apiece. I did this every day. It was just unbelievable, the bread lines. The only thing I could compare it with was Germany in 1922. It looked like there was no tomorrow. . . .

Sidney J. Weinberg
Senior partner, Goldman-Sachs Company, a leading invest-ment house. He served during [Franklin Delano] Roosevelt's first two Administrations as an industrial adviser.

October 29, 1929—I remember that day very intimately. I stayed in the office a week without going home. The tape was running, I've forgotten how long that night. It must have been ten, eleven o'clock before we got the final reports. It was like a thunder clap. Everybody was stunned. Nobody knew what it was all about. The Street had general confusion. They didn't understand it any more than anybody else. They thought something would be announced.

Prominent people were making statements. John D. Rockefeller, Jr., announced on the steps of J.P. Morgan, I think, that he and his sons were buying common stock. Immediately, the market went down again. Pools combined to support the market, to no avail. The public got scared and sold. It was a very trying period for me. Our investment company went up to two, three hundred, and then went down to practically nothing. As all investment companies did.

Over-speculation was the cause, a reckless disregard of economics. There was a group ruthlessly selling short. You could sell anything and depress the market unduly. The more you depressed it, the more you created panic. Today we have protections against it. Call money [repayable on demand] went up—was it twenty percent?

No one was so sage that he saw this thing coming. You can be a Sunday morning quarterback. A lot of people have said afterwards, "I saw it coming, I sold all my securities." There's a credibility gap there. There are always some people who are conservative, who did sell out. I didn't know any of these.

I don't know anybody that jumped out of the window.

But I know many who threatened to jump. They ended up in nursing homes and insane asylums and things like that. These were people who were trading in the market or in banking houses. They broke down physically, as well as financially.

Roosevelt saved the system. It's trite to say the system would have gone out the window. But certainly a lot of institutions would have changed. We were on the verge of something. You could have had a rebellion; you could have had a civil war. . . .

You had no governmental control of margins, so people could buy on a shoestring.

A Depression could not happen again, not to the extent of the one in '29. Unless inflation went out of hand and values went beyond true worth. A deep stock market reaction could bring a Depression, yes. There would be immediate Government action, of course. A moratorium. But in panic, people sell regardless of worth. Today you've got twenty-odd million stockholders owning stock. At that time you had probably a million and a half. You could have a sharper decline now than you had in 1929.

Most of the net worth of people today is in values. They haven't got it in cash. In a panic, values go down regardless of worth. A house worth $30,000, the minute you have a panic, isn't worth anything. Everybody feels good because the stock they bought at fifty is now selling at eighty. So they have a good feeling. But it's all on paper. . . .

John Hersch
He is the senior partner in a large brokerage house in Chicago. From his LaSalle Street office, on this late afternoon we can see the crowds below, worrying toward buses and parking lots, heading home.

"It's been a fascinating business for me right from 1924 to 1968. I've been in it a long time, and I'm very proud of it. It's entirely different than it was in the Twenties. The canons of ethics are extremely strict. There are still bad episodes once in a while, but it's a big society."

His is an air of worldly-weariness.

I came into the business, out of the University of

Chicago, about Christmas, 1924. I had about $3,000 in the stock market, which was all the money I had. On Black Friday—Thursday, was it?—that margin account went out of the window. I may have had about $62 left.

My wife had a colossal $125 a week job with a Shakespearean theater company. That night, she came home to our little apartment, and she said, "Guess what happened today?" I said, "What?" She said, "I quit." I was making about $60 a week and she was making $125. Two-thirds of our income and all of our savings disappeared that day.

I was a margin clerk. He's a man who keeps the figures on individual accounts, if they're carrying stocks on margin—that is, if they're carrying stocks without paying for them.

When the break started, you had a deluge of selling, from weakened margin accounts. We had to stay up all night figuring. We'd work till one o'clock and go to the LaSalle Hotel and get up about five and get some breakfast and continue figuring margin accounts. 'Cause everybody was in trouble. But everybody.

The guy I worked for was sitting in the wire room, watching the tape. The tape was something to see, because Radio Corporation, let's say, would be ninety-five on the tape . . . they'd flash you sixty on the floor. The floor was a madhouse. I said to him: "Are we solvent?" He says, "I won't know till about twelve tonight." He was half-serious. It was brutal.

The Crash—it didn't happen in one day. There were a great many warnings. The country was crazy. Everybody was in the stock market, whether he could afford it or not. Shoeshine boys and waiters and capitalists. . . . A great many holding company pyramids were unsound, really fictitious values. Mr. Insull was a case in point. It was a mad dream of get-rich-quick.

The Crash—it didn't happen in one day. There were a great many warnings.

It wasn't only brokers involved in margin accounts. It was banks. They had a lot of stinking loans. The banks worked in as casual a way as the brokers did. And when they folded. . . .

I had a friend in Cincinnati who was young and attractive. He had a wife and children and he was insured for $100,000. Life was over as far as he was concerned. He took a dive, to take care of his wife and kids. There was a number who took the dive, to collect on insurance policies. It's unthinkable now, when you know how many people have been able to come back.

There were others that impress me. I kept hearing about town that their businesses were in trouble. But they never lowered their standard of living a bit. They lived like kings, right through the Depression. I've never been able to figure this out. I knew some people who maintained their Lake Shore Drive apartments and cars, and everybody knew they were in trouble. I never knew how they did it, and I didn't care particularly. My friends and I were all broke, and we had no pretensions.

You had no governmental control of margins, so people could buy on a shoestring. And when they began pulling the plug . . . you had a deluge of weakness. You also had short-selling and a lack of rules.[3] There were many cases of staid, reputable bankers making securities available on special deals—below the market price—for their friends. Anything went, and everything did go.

Today, there are very few bankers of any repute who have objected to the Securities Exchange Commission (SEC). They believe that the regulation in 1933 was a very, very sound thing for our business.

Life After the Crash

In '32 and '33, there was no securities business to speak of. We played a lot of bridge in the afternoons on LaSalle Street. There was nobody to call or see. It was so quiet, you could hear a certificate drop. (Laughs.) Nobody was making a living. A lot of them managed to eke out $40, $60 a week, but mostly we played bridge. (Laughs.)

I found a certain obtuseness about what's going on in the country. Even after it happened. Of course, at the beginning of the New Deal, the capitalists embraced Franklin Roosevelt as a real savior of our system. The Chicago *Tribune* wrote laudatory articles about him. Editorials. As soon as things got a little better, the honeymoon was over. You know

---

3. "Now under SEC rules, you can only sell if the stock goes up an eighth. You can't sell it on the downtake."

all those old stories about guys getting on the train at Lake Forest: they were always looking for one headline every morning, that black headline about F.D.R. These people. . . .

It took this guy with the long cigarette holder to do some planning about basic things—like the SEC and the Works Progress Administration (WPA) and even the lousy Blue Eagle [the symbol of the Roosevelt administration's National Recovery Administration]. It put a new spirit in the country.

Chapter 3

The Aftermath

1
The Crash of 1929: The Slide into Depression

Edward Chancellor

In the following excerpt from his book *Devil Take the Hindmost: A History of Financial Speculation*, Edward Chancellor reviews both the immediate and the subsequent reaction to the stock market crash of 1929. Chancellor discusses the Hoover administration's attempts to mitigate the damage and restore confidence. The author also describes the Roosevelt administration's assault on speculation and describes what happened to many of the decade's notorious speculators. According to Chancellor, many measures taken in response to the crash were a result of the economic theories of economist John Maynard Keynes, who blamed laissez-faire capitalism for the crash, urging government control. In addition, Chancellor summarizes other theories historians and economists have developed to explain the crash and the Great Depression that followed. Chancellor is also a freelance contributor to *The Financial Times of London* and *The Economist*.

A merica faced its stock market ordeal with a sense of humour. The market steadied the day after Black Tuesday when John D. Rockefeller, Sr., announced that he and his son were purchasing "sound common stocks." "Sure," replied Eddie Cantor from the Broadway footlights, himself down a reported million dollars, "who else had any money left?"[42] It was Cantor who gave publicity to the suicide legends of two speculators leaping from a bridge holding hands because they shared a joint account, and of hotel reception clerks asking new arrivals whether they came to sleep or to jump.* He also observed that since the Crash women's hemlines had come down. The Jazz Age, according to Scott Fitzgerald, had "leapt to a spectacular death." More austere times were around the corner.

Although stocks continued to slide until the middle of November, Hoover's administration acted promptly to mitigate the fallout from the Crash. The President's public pronouncements were consistently upbeat. He convened business leaders and urged them to maintain wages in order to sustain demand; private and public organisations were asked to bring forward their construction plans; and Treasury Secretary Mellon announced a small tax cut in November. The banking authorities also acted speedily. On 31 October, the Federal Reserve reduced the discount rate to 5 percent (followed by a further reduction of half a percent two weeks later). The New York Federal Reserve Bank oversaw a massive shift in the call loan market, as outstanding margin loans dropped by 50 percent between September and November. Foreign and corporate lenders continued to withdraw their funds from the call loan market, and were replaced by the New York banks which maintained low rates on loans and reduced margin requirements to 25 percent. There were no significant banking or brokerage failures in the immediate aftermath of the Crash, apart from the Industrial Bank of Flint, Michigan, which was forced to close its doors after it was discovered that a cabal of employees had stolen $3.5 million and lost it in the stock market. American corporations also did their best to steady nerves. The day after Black Tuesday, U.S. Steel and several other companies announced increased dividends. Samuel Rosenwald of Sears, Roebuck and Samuel Insull declared they would guarantee their employees' margin accounts. When General Motors announced an extra dividend on 14 November, the news was greeted jubilantly and the Dow Jones stepped off its low of 198 and rose by nearly 25 percent over the next few days.

Optimism was quick to resurface. On the day the market turned, Baruch cabled Churchill to inform him that the financial crisis was over, although this was of little comfort

*Galbraith asserts that the stories of suicide associated with the Crash are myths. Yet the day after Black Thursday, Churchill wrote, "Under my window a gentleman cast himself down fifteen storeys and was dashed to pieces, causing a wild commotion and the arrival of the fire brigade." (Gilbert, *Churchill*, V, p. 350.)

to the future prime minister, who lost more than £10,000—
roughly £300,000 at today's values—in the Crash and was
obliged to live frugally for the next few years. Baruch's was a
conventional opinion shared by many of the smaller market
players who believed the Crash presented them with yet another buying opportunity. The news was mostly positive.
Turnover in the stock market was lively at five to six million
shares a day; many corporations announced record profits
for the previous year; and mergers in banking and utilities
continued, as did the property boom. People took comfort
in the fact that the major banks appeared well capitalised. In
New York, J.J. Raskob continued with his plans for the
hundred-storey Empire State Building, which he described
as a symbol for "a land which reached for the sky with its feet
on the ground."[43] In his ambition to build the world's tallest
building Raskob faced competition from his fellow speculator, Walter Chrysler, who was building his own 1,146-foot-
high skyscraper.* Meanwhile, William Crapo Durant busied
himself with new stock pools. In March 1930, President
Hoover announced that "the worst effects of the crash upon
employment will have passed during the next sixty days."[44]
The following month the Dow Jones broke through the 300
barrier, up nearly 50 percent from its post-Crash low.

Yet the "suckers' rally," as it was later called, came to an
end in the spring of 1930 and the market resumed its downward course until the summer of 1932, when the Dow
reached a low of 41.88 on a turnover of under 400,000
shares. In the intervening period, the country's gross national
product had fallen by 60 percent from its 1929 level, and unemployment had risen to twelve and a half million. Over a
third of the nonagricultural workforce was unemployed.

As the nation sank into depression, the apotheosis of the
businessman came to an end. In March 1932, Ivar Kreuger,
the Swedish Match King, committed suicide in a Paris hotel after his business empire collapsed under the weight of
debts and the discovery of Kreuger's own frauds. The following month, Samuel Insull's Middle West Utilities went

---

*The Chrysler Building provides the classic example of what economists half jok-
ingly call the "erection index." This predicts that the top of a bull market can be
called when the height of a new building exceeds all previous records. The erection
index has recently proved a reliable indicator, since the world's tallest building, the
Petronas Towers in Malaysia, was completed a few months before the onset of the
Asian crisis of 1997.

into bankruptcy, and Insull fled the county (he later returned to face trial and was acquitted of fraud.) The directors of the Goldman Sachs Trading Corporation were put on trial for wasting the company's assets. Charles Mitchell was forced to resign from the National City Bank, whose share price fell to 4 percent of its 1929 peak, and in 1934 he was tried for income tax evasion. William Crapo Durant was sold out by his brokers in late 1930 and declared bankrupt in 1936 with debts of nearly a million dollars. He found temporary employment washing dishes in a New Jersey restaurant. Jesse Livermore, who had made his first fortune in Wall Street during the 1907 panic, lost an estimated $32 million before being declared bankrupt in March 1934. Six years later, Livermore blew his brains out in the washroom of the Sherry-Netherland Hotel in New York. When the market touched bottom in 1932, Radio Corporation of America was selling for $2.50 a share, down from $114 three years earlier. Mike Meehan, the Radio specialist on the New York Stock Exchange, was reported to have lost $40 million in the Crash. His seats on the Exchange were put up for sale and his brokerage offices on the transatlantic liners were closed down. In 1936, Meehan entered a lunatic asylum.

Although stocks continued to slide until the middle of November, Hoover's administration acted promptly to mitigate the fallout from the Crash.

Popular history holds these men, along with their countless followers, responsible for the Great Depression. At his inauguration in March 1933, Franklin Delano Roosevelt addressed the nation:

> . . . Plenty is at our doorstep, but a generous use of it languishes in the very sight of the supply. Primarily this is because rulers of the exchange of mankind's goods have failed through their own stubbornness and their own incompetence, have admitted their failure, and have abdicated. Practices of the unscrupulous money changers stand indicted in the court of public opinion, rejected by the hearts and minds of men.

True they have tried, but their efforts have been cast in the pattern of an outworn tradition. Faced by the failure of credit they have proposed only lending of more money. Stripped of the lure of profit by which to induce our people to follow false leadership, they have resorted to exhortations, pleading tearfully to restore confidence. They know only the rules of a generation of self-seekers. They have no vision, and when there is no vision the people perish.

The money changers have fled from their high seats in the temple of our civilisation. We may now restore that temple to the ancient truths. The measure of the restoration lies in the extent to which we apply social values more noble than mere monetary profit.

Had Roosevelt referred to "speculators" rather than "money changers" his meaning might have been clearer, but as it was a time for divine retribution, with the new President playing the role of a wrathful Christ, the biblical "money changers" had a more suitable ring. Less than a year earlier, in the summer of 1932, Roosevelt had staked his claim to presidential office on the failure of economic individualism and the responsibility of Wall Street for the Depression. Hoover was stigmatised as an unfeeling, laissez-faire, new era Republican (an attack that unfairly overlooked Hoover's unceasing, if futile, attempts to revive the economy). In the spring of 1932, the Senate Committee on Banking and Currency opened its investigation into the operations of Wall Street during the 1920s. Ferdinand Pecora, the Sicilian-born head counsel for the investigation, interrogated the prominent financiers of the 1920s and mercilessly exposed their shortcomings. Tales of pools, market manipulation, preferential treatment for insiders, shoddy treatment of outsiders, tax evasion, and excessive remuneration were revealed to the public at the moment of its greatest distress. It was Pecora's conclusion that the Exchange had become "a glorified casino where the odds were heavily weighted against the eager outsiders."[45]

During Roosevelt's first administration a series of measures were initiated to restrict the freedom under which speculators had formerly operated. Investment and commercial banking were separated by the Glass-Steagall Act of

1933. In future, the capital of commercial banks and their ability to lend would no longer fluctuate with the rise and fall of the stock market, and their customers would no longer be pushed second-rate securities. A year later, the Securities Exchange Act became law. Stock market pools, insider trading, and market manipulation were proscribed. The Federal Reserve was given the power to restrict margin loans, which were limited to a maximum of 50 percent of the collateral value of shares. The Securities and Exchange Commission was established to police the capital markets and prevent "unnecessary, unwise and destructive speculation" (in a controversial move, Roosevelt appointed Joseph Kennedy, a member of numerous stock pools, as its first chairman). Bear speculators, whose short selling was blamed by nearly everyone, including Hoover, for the collapse in market confidence, were restricted by the introduction of the "uptick" rule, which permitted short sales only after a stock had risen on its last trade.

Tales of pools, market manipulation, preferential treatment for insiders, shoddy treatment of outsiders, tax evasion, and excessive remuneration were revealed to the public at the moment of its greatest distress.

The politics of Roosevelt's New Deal rejected the free-wheeling individualism of the 1920s and replaced it with governmental direction in economic affairs. In place of market forces came federal welfare, housing and work programmes, bank deposit insurance, prices and incomes policies, minimum wage legislation, and a number of other measures. Speculation, whether in stocks, bonds, land, or commodities, was no longer to play such a key role in economic life. These largely ad hoc measures were provided with an intellectual framework by the publication of Keynes's *The General Theory of Employment, Interest and Money* in 1936. Keynes attacked the earlier prominence given to speculators and the stock market in the allocation of capital resources. He asserted that "there is no clear evidence from [recent] experience that the investment policy which is socially advantageous coincides with that which is most profitable." In perhaps the most quoted passage from the book, Keynes wrote:

> Speculators may do no harm as bubbles on a steady stream of enterprise. But the position is serious when enterprise becomes a bubble on a whirlpool of specu- lation. When the capital development of a country be- comes a by-product of the activities of a casino, the job is likely to be ill done.[46]

In support of this statement, Keynes drew his readers' at- tention to the recent history of Wall Street, whose success in directing new investment towards the most profitable channels "cannot be claimed as one of the outstanding tri- umphs of *laissez-faire* capitalism." As a cure for the evil of speculation, he suggested a punitive capital gains tax on stock market transactions in order to force investors to take a long-term view. For the state, a body free from the "ani- mal spirits" that characterised the speculator and thus able to consider social advantages rather than mere profit, he foresaw a greater role as an investor. In Europe, at least, the age of nationalisation beckoned.

Not all economists and historians have been convinced by this scapegoating of speculators in the wake of the Crash. Milton Friedman, the monetarist economist, has claimed that "the stock market crash in 1929 was a momentous event, but it did not produce the Great Depression and it was not a major factor in the Depression's severity."[47] In- stead, Friedman (and his co-author Anna Schwartz in their *Monetary History of the United States)* blamed the Federal Re- serve for following an overly restrictive monetary policy which caused the stock of money to decline by a third be- tween August 1929 and March 1933. According to Fried- man and Schwartz, the Depression deepened after the first banking crisis in the autumn of 1930 when the Bank of the United States was (in their view) unnecessarily allowed to fail. This analysis appears to play down the degree to which the early major banking failures—of both the Detroit banks and the Bank of the United States—were largely due to their exposure to declining property prices and stock market losses at their securities affiliates. It was these failures which, in turn, triggered the general banking crisis. The experience of the Japanese banks after the bubble economy of the 1980s reinforces the impression that the banking crisis of 1932 was the direct result of the preceding era of speculation.

Charles Kindleberger, viewing events from a more international perspective, saw the Depression as the result of declining commodity prices (due to endemic overproduction since the First World War) and the failure of the United States to adopt the role as international lender of the last resort to European nations. In place of loans, the Hoover administration introduced tariffs which led swiftly to retaliation, followed by competitive currency devaluations across the world. Other economic historians have blamed the Depression on the rigidities caused by the gold exchange standard which operated during the 1920s and early 1930s.[48]

Murray Rothbard, the American economist, has argued that the policies of Herbert Hoover were to blame for the Great Depression, not for being too laissez-faire as Roosevelt asserted, but because they were insufficiently so. Hoover's essential failure, Rothbard claimed, was to ignore Treasury Secretary Mellon's advice that the Crash would be beneficial if it were allowed, in his oft-quoted phrase, to "liquidate labor, liquidate stocks, liquidate the farmers, liquidate real estate."[49] In other words, Mellon suggested that the market should be left to fall until it found its own clearing level when demand would return and the economy revive. Instead, Hoover's policies prevented wages from falling at a time when asset and commodity prices were declining. This served to increase unemployment and reduce the returns on capital, thus preventing reinvestment. Rothbard concluded that the "'guilt of the Great Depression must be lifted from the shoulders of the free market economy, and placed where it properly belongs: at the doors of politicians, bureaucrats, and the mass of 'enlightened' economists."[50]

The relationship between the Crash and the Great Depression is one of the most keenly debated issues in economic history.

As if this were not enough, Herbert Hoover blamed Franklin Roosevelt and the Democrats for deepening the public's fear and distrust throughout the election campaign of 1932 and for failing to cooperate with the outgoing administration's relief measures. Hoover has received recent support from Barrie Wigmore (in *The Crash and Its After-math*), who claimed that Roosevelt's speeches in 1932 and his refusal to guarantee the gold standard precipitated the public's hoarding of money and brought on the banking crisis of early 1933. Wigmore concludes that Roosevelt "as much as anyone, raised the Crash to its symbolic position as the cause of the Depression."[51]

The relationship between the Crash and the Great Depression is one of the most keenly debated issues in economic history. Because the debate is politically charged, concerning whether markets should ultimately be controlled by governments or left to their own devices, it will never be resolved to the satisfaction of all parties. As Roosevelt showed, political capital could be earned by insinuating a causal link between the Crash and the economic crisis. Subsequently, that link was used to justify the policies of the New Deal. A generation later, Professor Friedman's assertion that the stock market collapse did not cause the banking crisis or lead to the Great Depression was taken up fervidly by the Reagan Republicans who wished to overturn Roosevelt's legacy.

We find from the record of contemporaries that the Crash and the subsequent decline in asset values had a profound effect on people's expectations. In an essay entitled "Echoes from the Jazz Age" (first published in *Scribner's Magazine* in November 1931), Scott Fitzgerald claimed that the Jazz Age ended with the Crash. The "most expensive orgy in history" was over

> because the utter confidence which was its essential prop received an enormous jolt, and it didn't take long for the flimsy structure to settle earthward . . . It was borrowed time anyhow—the whole upper tenth of the nation living with the insouciance of grand ducs and the casualness of call girls.[52]

As the market crashed, the happy vision of the future dispelled, leaving the American people uncertain and unprepared for the difficult economic conditions of the early 1930s. In *Only Yesterday*, Frederick Lewis Allen saw the Depression as a "profound psychological reaction from the exuberance of 1929":

> Prosperity is more than an economic condition; it is a state of mind. The Big Bull Market had been more

than the climax of a cycle in American mass thinking and mass emotion. There was hardly a man or woman in the country whose attitude toward life had not been affected by it in some degree and was not now affected by the sudden and brutal shattering of hope. With the Big Bull Market gone and prosperity going, Americans were soon to find themselves living in an altered world which called for new adjustments, new ideas, new habits of thought, and a new order of values.[53]

During the late 1920s, American economic reality had become dependent on a precarious vision of the future. After the Crash, when every tenet of the new era philosophy was shown to be false, Americans lost that confidence in the future which is necessary for the successful operation of the economic system. As George Orwell observed, "poverty annihilates the future." When asset values declined, causing havoc in the banking system, a psychology of fear replaced the optimism of the previous decade. Perhaps, as some claimed, the Roaring Twenties were morally degenerate years deserving of a biblical visitation; but they were also a period when people exhibited a capacity for dreaming, a faith in the future, an entrepreneurial appetite for risk, and a belief in individual freedom. These profoundly American traits took a severe knocking in October 1929 and appeared to be extinguished during the Great Depression. They would return.

Notes

42. Eddie Cantor, *Caught Short! A Saga of Wailing Wall Street* [1929] (repr. Burlington, Vt., 1992), p. 22
43. Thomas and Morgan-Witts, *Bubble*, p. 368.
44. Noyes, *Market Place*, p. 342.
45. Pecora, *Wall Street*, p. 260.
46. Keynes, *General Theory*, p. 159.
47. Cited by C.P. Kindleberger, *The World in Depression 1929–39* (London, 1987), p. 106.
48. See Peter Temin, *Lessons from the Great Depression* (Cambridge, Mass., 1990).
49. Hoover, *Memoirs*, III, p. 30.
50. Murray Rothbard, *America's Great Depression* (Princeton, 1963), p. 295.
51. Wigmore, *Crash and Its Aftermath*, p. 337.
52. F. Scott Fitzgerald, *The Crack-Up* (ed. Edmund Wilson, New York, 1945), p. 21.
53. Allen, *Only Yesterday*, p. 338.

2

Wall Street Does Not Determine Prosperity

New Republic

At the time of the stock market crash of 1929, opinions about its impact on the economy varied. While some believed the crash signaled an equally devastating business depression, others believed that America's economy was fundamentally sound. The editors of the *New Republic*, a journal of opinion on political and cultural issues, argue that contrary to accepted opinion, Wall Street is not a barometer of business prosperity. In the following article published on November 6, 1929, the editors of the *New Republic* explain why the traditional assumptions about the relationship between the stock market and business conditions no longer apply. For example, the editors argue that, although speculators may once have made stock purchases based upon future profits, speculators in the booming market bought shares to profit from a swiftly rising market, which had little to do with business profits. The editors also discuss changes in the traditional role of credit and the current status of production, concluding that the Wall Street crash should not seriously impact the national prosperity. Whether or not the arguments made by the editors were tenable, the Great Depression that followed the crash revealed that the American economy was not as sound as believed.

The crash in stock prices concerned a great many people directly because of their holdings, past or present, but not so many as has been popularly supposed. Bootblacks, barbers and elevator boys have undoubtedly been dabbling in speculation, but by no means all of them; and tens of millions of cotton textile workers, farmers, school teachers—the rank and file of the country—have never been able to afford this fascinating game. Most of us are, however, indirectly concerned because of the possible portent which the market may exhibit of future conditions in industry and trade.

It used to be thought that the course of stock prices was a pretty accurate barometer of business prosperity, anticipating general business conditions, by about six months. Experience, it was supposed, had indicated this to be the case. Some have accepted this rule-of-thumb as an unexplained superstition, but if we are to judge whether we may now expect a business depression of the same order as the Wall Street panic, we must inquire what well founded reasons there were for the correspondence, and whether they still exist.

One explanation rested upon the collective judgment of stockholders and speculators concerning the business future. Many of them knew, it was believed, what were the prospects of the companies in whose shares they were dealing. When a man bought stock, it was because he expected business profits to increase. When more wanted to buy than wanted to sell, that drove stock prices up; when more wanted to sell than wanted to buy, that drove stock prices down. The course of stock prices was, therefore, a sort of election return, promptly registering the opinion of a majority of investors and speculators concerning future profits. And the opinion of that majority was supposed to be more sound than the opinion of any individual.

It used to be thought that the course of stock prices was a pretty accurate barometer of business prosperity.

Clearly, this explanation does not fit the recent facts of the market. For many months—even perhaps for several years—speculators have been buying stock without regard to the prospect of business profits. The prices at which most stocks sold were already so high that any conceivable profits within six months or so would not justify a person in holding them for the sake of current dividends. An investor who bought shares to hold for any considerable length of time did so because of the growth in profits which he expected over a period of years. And most persons who bought shares did not plan to keep them, but to resell at a higher price. The gain was to come, not out of dividends, but out of the price inflation of a boom market. The market's election return had very little to do with any expectation of business profits within a short period; any competent observer could register a better judgment concerning the short-term business future, by paying careful attention to the now voluminous statistics concerning production, trade and earnings—matters pretty much ignored by Wall Street's customers.

The Role of Credit

Another explanation of the old parallelism had to do with credit. If credit was abundant, and interest rates were low, both business and Wall Street benefitted. Business activity increased, and so did speculation. *Per contra*, when credit was restricted and interest rates rose, both business and speculation suffered. Since the effect of credit conditions on business activity was somewhat delayed, whereas it was felt promptly in Wall Street, the behavior of stock prices would anticipate that of business. Whatever truth there was in this theory has only a limited application to the present situation. Credit began to be restricted and interest rates to rise long before the stock market crash. With an inflated and booming market, speculators did not care how much they had to pay for loans wherewith they carried their stocks; they expected to resell soon enough and at sufficiently higher prices so that they could afford to pay the interest. The high rates prevailing for security loans did somewhat affect the interest charged on money lent for other purposes, but to nothing like the same extent. Except in building construction, which relies heavily on credit and probably was somewhat retarded by tight money, production went forward at an unprecedented pace in most of our major industries, all through the period of credit stringency. Most great industries either did not need bank loans, because of the abundance of working capital which they had secreted out of their large profits, or sold stock in sufficient quantities to allow them to proceed. In deed, much of the money lent "on call" [payable on demand] at the high rate prevailing in Wall Street came from the surplus funds of large business corporations themselves. And when the final crash came, interest rates had fallen considerably.

A somewhat allied theory accounted for the relationship between stock prices and business by the explanation of the business cycle which attributes it to a general inflation and deflation. When credit inflation seizes business, prices of commodities begin to rise. This stimulates production in advance of demand. For a while the wheels hum—as they did in 1919 and 1920. But production goes ahead faster than the products can be sold and used by the public. Inventories are built up which become unsaleable when prices begin to fall, profits to vanish, production to decrease and unemployment to reduce the purchasing power of the consumers. Stock prices, being more sensitive than commodity prices, but being affected by much the same influences, anticipate the inflation and deflation of business. But business has not exhibited any such phenomena in the period of the recent Wall Street boom. Prices of commodities have not risen. So far as we know, unsaleable inventories have not been built up. The policy of "hand-to-mouth" purchasing has been fairly well established. There is no particular reason to expect a precipitous drop in commodity prices, analogous to that which has depressed the prices of shares.

It is difficult to see how the Wall Street crash can seriously affect general prosperity, or even foretell its fate.

In view of these considerations it is difficult to see how the Wall Street crash can seriously affect general prosperity, or even foretell its fate, any more than did the collapse of the Florida boom. It may depress those lines of business whose customers consisted chiefly of successful bull speculators [who expect prices to rise]—but these are strictly limited in area and importance. It might conceivably shake that "confidence" of businessmen which is supposed to play such a large part in their activity, but it would be astonishing if many businessmen in their senses had placed more reliance upon the mystic influence of a runaway stock market than they do upon a stream of orders coming from their sales departments. On the other hand, the collapse of the stock boom will release money and credit for productive purposes. It might conceivably aid real estate and building construction.

Whether such prosperity as we have been enjoying will proceed without interruption may be uncertain, but it depends upon quite a different set of considerations. It depends upon whether the demand for building will continue in its recent volume, or will fall away to much lower levels. It depends upon whether the automobile manufacturers will be able to find a market in the future for as many cars as they have been making—either at home or abroad. It depends upon whether we can go on financing a growing volume of exports by means of foreign loans; whether international trade as a whole may be expected to grow, or to be discouraged by higher tariffs. It depends upon whether we can adjust our resources of capital and labor to the needs of the population with as little waste as possible. It depends upon whether, as we increase our productivity of goods intended for widespread consumption, we similarly increase the real wages and purchasing power of those who are expected to consume them. It depends more upon a hundred other factors than it does upon the disappointed calculations of those who fatuously expected stock prices to go on rising to the zenith, without any relationship to the earning capacity of the properties whose ownership shares of stock are supposed to represent.

3

Hoover Takes Action

Albert U. Romasco

Although Herbert Hoover is often remembered as an advocate of the philosophy that economic problems are best left to resolve themselves, he actually maintained that the government had a role in mitigating the results of the stock market crash of 1929, writes history professor Albert U. Romasco in the following excerpt from his book *The Poverty of Abundance: Hoover, the Nation, the Depression.* Although Hoover reassured the American people that the status of the nation's economy was fundamentally sound, Hoover also knew that his administration must act to restore confidence and stimulate business. Hoover immediately gathered the nation's business leaders to obtain their commitment to minimize rather than broaden the impact of the crash by continuing with business as usual rather than cutting orders, inventories, and wages, says Romasco. Hoover depended on their voluntary cooperation, however, and did little to alter the economic conditions and institutions that many argue contributed to the depression that followed.

O n Thursday morning, October 24, 1929, "the great bull market," [in which prices are expected to rise], of the 1920's came to an end. In time, the events of this and subsequent days on the New York Stock Exchange would be identified simply as "the Great Crash." Later, as the panic developed into a definite depression, this period quickly became known as "the Great Depression." For Americans, these October days marked the close of that buoyant interlude, "the New Era." But for Hoover and the American sys-

Excerpted from "The Stock Market Crash: Hoover's Initial Program" in *The Poverty of Abundance: Hoover, the Nation, the Depression* by Albert U. Romasco. Copyright © 1965 by Albert U. Romasco. Reprinted by permission of Oxford University Press.

tem, these dramatic developments posed a grave and immediate challenge.

Panics and depressions dotted the American past from its earliest days as a nation onward; they were no new affliction. Nor had these periodic disruptions of the nation's economic equilibrium occurred without an accompaniment of loud lamentations—fervent importunities for federal aid. Yet those who clamored for this assistance clamored in vain: they were heard and ignored by a long succession of Presidents. From the presidency of Martin Van Buren to that of Woodrow Wilson, the administrations which confronted depressions refrained from any direct official action. President Warren Harding, faced with the economic collapse of 1920–21, seemed to break with this tradition. He called a national conference on unemployment in 1921, which conducted extensive and valuable inquiries, and made numerous recommendations on appropriate action. But the federal government was not to carry out these proposals; it was the nation's mayors who were urged to act. Little was accomplished. The precedent of presidential inactivity in depression times—waiting unobtrusively for recovery—remained essentially unimpaired.

The Laissez-Faire Philosophy

One theory held that depressions were best met by patient forbearance. Temporary dislocations were to be overcome not by artificial, governmental tinkering, but through a natural process of readjustment. Supported by the authority of Adam Smith, and reinforced by the Spencerian rationalization of biological evolution to economic affairs, the theory was further buttressed by American antipathy to centralized, governmental direction and control. By 1929 this mixture of theory, experience, and tradition had become diffused into a habit of mind. It was as a habit that this outlook achieved its widest influence. "The great advantage of allowing nature to take her course," Stuart Chase pointed out caustically, "is that it obviates thought. . . . There is no need to think, no need to take concrete action. Just sit and wait with folded hands."

Among members of President Herbert Hoover's official family, Secretary of the Treasury Andrew Mellon best exemplified this trait. After the stock market collapse of late October 1929, Mellon emerged as the spokesman and leader of one school of thought within the administration. Mellon counseled non-interference by the government. In his view, the federal government was to stand passively aside while inflated values were liquidated and the economic situation readjusted itself to normal. The Secretary of the Treasury expressed the liquidationist position perfectly with his simple, brutal formula: "Liquidate labor, liquidate stocks, liquidate the farmers, liquidate real estate." It was advice that curiously blended fatalistic and optimistic elements—fatalistic in that it condemned any effort by the government to cushion the reverberations of the crash as futile; optimistic because it believed that an unimpeded liquidation would be brief and beneficial.

Temporary dislocations were to be overcome not by artificial, governmental tinkering, but through a natural process of readjustment.

President Hoover disagreed with this uncompromising laissez-faire viewpoint. Supported by others within his administration, he maintained that the shock of the market debacle should be cushioned and confined by the use of governmental authority. "To our minds," he later wrote, "the prime needs were to prevent bank panics such as had marked the earlier slumps, to mitigate the privation among the unemployed and the farmers which would certainly ensue." Publicly, the President attempted to allay precisely this same apprehension among the people over the probable consequences of the stock break. In answer to questions as to the possible effect of the crash on the nation's prosperity, at a press conference on October 25, 1929, he made the celebrated declaration that "the fundamental business of the country, that is production and distribution of commodities, is on a sound and prosperous basis." He repeated this reassuring view on November 15 by stating that "any lack of confidence in the economic future or the basic strength of business in the United States is foolish." Many people at the time applauded these remarks and the intent behind them, including the *Nation*, which in a short time was to be a consistent and severe critic of Hoover. "The great task of the next few months." it now wrote, "is the restoration of confidence—confidence in the fundamental strength of the financial structure notwithstanding the strain that has been put upon it, confidence in the essential soundness of legitimate industry and trade."

Yet, in spite of the sweeping nature of his assurances, Hoover did not delude himself about their complete efficacy. His own experience, he said, had taught him "that words are not of any great importance in times of economic disturbance. It is action," he insisted, "that counts." What line of action had he in mind?

The President suggested emergency Federal Reserve policies to establish a sound basis of stable credit and ample capital. He called for the stimulation of business activity by a combined policy of tax reductions, the revival of construction work, and expanded exports. Above all else, he insisted that the success of this program would require "the co-ordination of business and governmental agencies in concerted action. . . ." This last suggestion was the very heart of his program. To aid in achieving this essential coordination, Hoover announced his intention of calling a series of conferences with the leaders of the nation's major economic interests. . . .

Hoover stressed the immense challenge that the nation's deranged economy presented the business community. "A great responsibility and a great opportunity," he declared gravely, "rest upon the business and economic organization of the country."

The Outcome of Prosperity

We might, at this point, re-examine briefly the major features and the underlying assumptions involved in Hoover's evaluation of the stock market crash and his program for dealing with it. According to popular opinion, past experience taught that a stock market crash signaled an impending depression. But, also, a severe decline in new construction invariably preceded a market collapse. While new construction was partly dependent on the need for new facilities, it was even more dependent upon the availability of low-interest, long-term credit. Yet, whenever a booming stock market existed, this credit became increasingly more difficult to come by. The more prolonged the bull market the more effectively it monopolized the sources of available surplus credit.

This absorption of credit was one consequence of the spectacular earnings in common stocks, which in turn forced credit rates gradually up to a level where only the expectation of spectacular returns would justify borrowing. In time, the high-interest rate—particularly on loans on the call-money [repayable on demand] market—came to represent a curiously mixed symbol of expectation and apprehension. The high-interest rate registered the sanguine expectations for the future; simultaneously it worked to deny funds for basic economic activities essential to sustain those future expectations. The inevitable crash was merely a matter of time.

Hoover stressed the immense challenge that the nation's deranged economy presented the business community.

The heritage of this way of thinking has been reflected in the ambivalent American attitude toward prosperity ever since. Periods of prosperity are anticipated with pleasure and, once achieved, enjoyed with apprehension. The immediate post–World War II years are a nice illustration of this complex interplay of expectations—recorded especially well in the pages of *Fortune*. Prosperity invariably fosters unreasonable expectation, thereby inducing inflationary pressure; and this outcome is largely responsible for the eventual undoing of prosperity. Prosperity, then, undergoes the transition from vigor to decay by the excessive growth of its original components. Prosperity, it appears, is much like happiness: elusive of control and when pursued too vigorously ending in disappointment.

Although past experience taught the sobering lesson that the ultimate outcome of prosperity was depression, it suggested also a more hopeful corollary: that is, the eventual outcome of depression was in turn a new period of prosperity. Moreover, experience, such as the most recent panic-depression cycle of 1920–21, indicated that the process of recovery followed roughly the reverse course of the crash-depression process. After the painful but necessary liquidation of inflated values, money and credit were released from the deflated market. Investors with surplus or idle capital, once convinced that the bottom of the deflationary spiral had been reached, cautiously sought new investment opportunities. This renewed willingness to invest might be described as the outward sign of an inward state of mind— "confidence." And confidence, like investment, is always based upon optimistic future expectations.

Such moderate expectation and revived confidence in future prospects, this reasoning held, completely altered the long-term credit market. Now, with ample funds at reasonable rates available once again, construction revived. And for observers sensitive to the operation of the business cycle, the construction revival was the first sign of the upward swing.

Hoover was thoroughly familiar with this frame of thought. But, while Hoover agreed with much of the accepted wisdom on business cycles, he disagreed completely with the major premise of the deflationists; that is, he rejected their assumption that business cycles were "natural" and thus unavoidable. The intelligence of man might mitigate even this scourge. The proof of his disagreement was the initial program he worked out immediately after the collapse of the great bull market. In effect, the President's program was an attempt to arrest the downward plunge of the business cycle at its very inception. He meant to short-circuit the familiar pattern of the past before it could develop in all its paralyzing ramifications. This ambitious undertaking might be achieved, it was thought, if two major objectives could be realized.

Abandoning Conventional Wisdom

Hoover had to convince businessmen that the familiar pattern of response, based upon the lessons of the past, could now be safely abandoned. In fact, some of the old maxims had to be disregarded so that they would not come about. Businessmen, whenever convinced that deflation was imminent, acted in a manner which accelerated the downward swing of the economy. They retrenched. Inventories and orders were cut. Prices were reduced. The work force was pared. And those fortunate enough to hold their jobs worked at a lower wage scale. Businessmen, in a word, liquidated. They liquidated in anticipation of a severe deflation, thereby making a reality the very state of affairs they feared and from which they sought security. Economically they scurried to their storm cellars.

This behavior, and the climate of opinion it confessed, proved highly contagious. Everyone—wholesalers, retailers, manufacturers—retrenched. The result was another twist of the screw downward: inventories were cut, orders were cut, production was cut, wages and employment were cut, purchasing power and consumption were cut. And on and on it went in a vicious downward spiral where every cautious measure grasped to achieve personal security only acted to sap the security of everyone. This spiral—especially in such a highly complex and intricately interdependent economic structure as ours—could continue until only the very strongest business, banking, and industrial units survived. It would end only when confidence was restored. And confidence would not revive until businessmen somehow decided that the downward spiral had reached bottom. "No one cares," as one editor tersely explained the dilemma, "to make commitments as long as there is a chance that the price paid today may be less tomorrow."

Periods of prosperity are anticipated with pleasure and, once achieved, enjoyed with apprehension.

It was this nightmare that Hoover foresaw and wanted to avoid. If businessmen could be persuaded to retain confidence in the basic soundness of the economy, the impulse toward caution and retrenchment would be minimized. The presidential business conferences were designed to promote these ends. In addition, the conferences were meant to ensure that businessmen acted in a fashion which would maintain stability. Instead of retrenching, they were to proceed with business as usual. Instead of anticipating trouble, they were to behave as if conditions were normal. And by pledging to maintain wages, prices, and employment they would minimize rather than augment the potential deflationary impact of the market collapse. "It was," as Walter Lippmann remarked, "an open conspiracy not to deflate."

Hoover's second major objective was to stimulate construction—that harbinger of a new period of prosperity. The National Business Survey Conference was created primarily for this purpose. The cure would not be left to exert itself only after a disastrous delay and through chance; it was to be applied at once by artificial means. The combination of these factors—confidence, business as usual, expanded construction—would shorten the downward phase of the business cycle from a prolonged period to a matter of months. "The conception behind this policy," economist George Soule noted, "was that the stock-market crash was an isolated affair, and business could be quarantined against its effects.". . .

> *By pledging to maintain wages, prices, and employment [business leaders] would minimize rather than augment the potential deflationary impact of the market collapse.*

Hoover wanted to prevent the stock market crash—for which he was not responsible—from triggering a depression. But good intentions cannot of themselves solve such problems. The crucial test was whether his program would work.

Yet, curiously, the success or failure of Hoover's program was almost wholly outside his direct control. For despite the fact that Hoover had been far more active than previous Presidents faced with a depression crisis, his initial program hardly committed the federal government to a major role in meeting the nation's danger. The President's role was actually confined to that of an influential adviser and well-placed cheerleader. The President's function was pointing the way to others, who, prodded on by encouragement from the White House, would provide the necessary leadership and energy to implement his ideas. The brunt of his program rested on the nation's traditional institutions. Combined by mutual pledges and a common aim, they were to act in a concert of good will and co-operation to surmount a major economic crisis.

The Role of Business Leaders

Among these institutions, the chief burden was undoubtedly put upon business leadership. Business leaders, aided by the positive help of the banks and the negative help of the labor unions, were to ensure that business proceeded as usual. Assisted by the cities, the states, and the federal government, they were to spearhead the movement to expand construction. Meanwhile, the existing private and public social welfare agencies were to care for whatever unemployment these measures failed to prevent. Hoover believed that the nation's traditional institutions, inspired with new vigor and the will to co-operate, were sufficient and capable to meet the challenge.

In considering Hoover's response to the crash during these first months, one is struck by the total absence of reform proposals. Hoover's program did not require change but a new spirit within existing institutions. While the collapse itself and its potential repercussions were not minimized, the need for structural changes in the nation's traditional economic arrangements—which had permitted such a devastating collapse—was completely neglected. The operations of the securities exchange, for example, with its esoteric practices—short-selling, margin accounts, investment trusts, inside and outside pools, bear raids, and call loans—were not to be probed for weakness and strengthened by reforms. Instead of reform, the stock market was to be immunized from the healthy body economic. There was, in other words, no assurance or indication that Hoover's program would protect the nation against a similar recurrence in the future.

Hoover believed that the nation's traditional institutions, inspired with new vigor and the will to co-operate, were sufficient and capable to meet the challenge.

Hoover's optimistic assumption may well explain why one of the nation's most important institutions was excluded from participation in his program. Since investigation and reform were not called for, there was no need for legislation. Congress had no apparent place in the ambitious plans of a Republican President. During these early months of domestic crisis, Congress was in session, but Hoover showed no inclination to enlist its aid. With Congress excluded, and the role of the presidency confined to inspiration and exhortation, the authority and power of the federal government could not be said to be committed in any direct sense.

This was precisely what Hoover wanted. It was not desirable, in the President's scale of values, that the crisis should be met by federal intervention. It was much more desirable that it should be met and overcome by the institutions which he had called upon, and this task was to be accomplished voluntarily by co-operative effort. In these first months, Hoover made the issue clear. The nation's institutions were challenged. All that remained was the test: were these institutions capable of overcoming a major, domestic economic crisis by voluntary co-operative action?

4

Helping President Hoover Restore Confidence

Will Rogers

Will Rogers was an entertainer and writer who wove humorous political commentary into his act and his writings. He dressed as a cowboy and is often remembered for his claim that "All I know is what I read in the newspaper." In the following excerpt from *The Autobiography of Will Rogers*, Rogers, a Democrat, uses his political humor to question the Hoover administration's ability to "restore confidence" in the nation's economy. Rogers, who had been advised to sell his stock before the crash, challenges the claim that those who lost money in the stock market crash, many of whom were his friends, only lost money on paper. He also claims that Americans should not look to the stock market as a measure of prosperity and questions the logic of encouraging stock speculation, which Rogers believes is akin to gambling.

I have been trying my best to help Mr. Hoover and Wall Street "Restore Confidence." You take confidence, its one of the hardest things in the World to get restored once it gets out of bounds. I have helped restore a lot of things in my time, such as cattle back to the home range. Herded Ziegfield Folly Girls toward the stage door near show time. Helped to revive interest in National Political Conventions. Even assisted the Democrats in every forlorn pilgrimage, and a host of other worthy charities. But I tell you this "Restoring Confidence" is the toughest drive I ever assisted in. When I took up the work two or three weeks ago, confidence was at a mighty low ebb, that is so all the Papers and speakers was saying.

Interpreting the Trouble on Wall Street

Wall Street had gone into one tail spin after another. You would pick up a paper in the morning and read the stock report and you wouldent think there was that many "Minus" signs in the world. Well the effect of it was just like going to Monte Carlo and hearing that everybody was betting on the Black and the Red had been coming up continually for two days. That would just simply demoralize southern France and the whole Riviera. Well thats what this Market was doing here. It was just taking all the joy out of gambling. If it kept on like that it would discourage Gambling, and that of course would be bad for the country (thats what they said).

I tell em that this country is bigger than Wall Street, and if they don't believe it, I show em the map.

Course there was a lot of us dumb ones that couldent understand it. We said, "Well if somebody lost money there, why somebody else must have made it. You cant just lose money to nobody, unless you drop it somewhere and nobody ever finds it." They then said a good deal of the money was "Lost on Paper." That is it was figures but it wasent real money. Well I had done that, I could remember every contract I would get for a seasons work on the stage or screen, my wife and I would sit down and figure out what all we would have by the end of that season. Well at the end of the season we had the figures but we couldent find the money. So Wall Street Men had nothing on us. In fact I dont think it had anything on anybody, for we all can take a piece of paper and if you give us enough pencils we can figure ourselves out a pretty neat little fortune in no time, so when I heard that most of the money had been lost on "Paper Profits," why I felt right at home with them.

But then everybody said it would have a demoralizing

effect on the country for so many to have their paper Profits all rubbed out at once. That it would have the effect of making people more careful with their money, and thereby make it bad for speculation. That if people dident trade in stock why Wall Street couldent exist.

So I says what can we do for em so they will keep on existing? "Why restore confidence." And thats what I been doing for weeks, writing and talking. Course I havent been buying anything myself. I wanted to give all the other folks a chance to have confidence first. There is none of the Greedy Pig about me. This confidence was for sale and I wanted them to have the very first chance of buying it.

Course I never could understand what the price of the stock had to do with keeping the company working and turning out their product. For instance if "Consolidated Corn Salve" stock had all been sold, and the company had that money it had brought in and was operating on that, what difference did it make to them if the stock was selling at a thousand bucks, or if people was using the stock to kindle their fire with? Their business was still to keep after those corns. In other words they should be watching corns instead of the market. If the shares sold for 564 one day and $1.80 the next, what had happened during the night to the afflicted toes of the country? Well I couldent get that.

Getting Right Back into the Market

Course they explained it off some way. Said, "Trading was good for the country, and kept things a circulating." So I finally went over to their side. I really did it for vanity, for I could see all the big men over there, and I felt flattered when I saw that I was one to join in this great work of getting people back to contributing to Wall street again. Course there is a lot of them that is going to take me time to get back. They not only lost confidence but they lost money, some of them all of their money (and it wasn't "Paper Money" they lost). So we will have to wait till they get some money in some other business, perhaps in some business in which they really have no confidence. Then they will be able to get back into the market not only with new confidence but new money. Thats going to take time in some cases.

But I am telling them that the Country as a whole is "Sound," and that all those who's heads are solid are bound to get back into the market again. I tell em that this country is bigger than Wall Street, and if they dont believe it, I show em the map.

Mr. Hoover called all the Railroad men in and they decided to do all they could to keep people from riding on Busses. Then he had all the Bankers there, and they announced what their annual Jip would be for the coming year. They agreed to be more careful in their loans, and see that the borrower dident buy a farm with it, as Agriculture was so uncertain. Try and get them to invest in some business where he could read the paper in the morning and see what he had. But its a great work, and I am just crazy about it. Viva confidence.

5

Business Confidence Has Been Reestablished

Herbert Hoover

Herbert Hoover had been president less than one year when the stock market crashed in 1929. Hoover hoped to stimulate business and restore confidence by enlisting the support of the nation's business leaders. In the following speech before the Senate and House of Representatives delivered on December 3, 1929, Hoover argues that the nation has enjoyed steady growth and prosperity during 1929, and to avoid the pessimism and fear that resulted from previous crashes, he has instituted voluntary cooperation from the business community to maintain wages and expand construction to insure continued consumption and reduce unemployment. Hoover claims that the banks remain strong and the government has taken action to improve problems in agriculture. Even with these measures, however, Hoover was unable to alleviate the unemployment, homelessness, and hunger that followed the stock market crash. Although Hoover encouraged state and local governments to support private charities, asked Congress to appropriate money for public-works projects, and backed the creation of the Reconstruction Finance Corporation (RFC), many blamed him for the worsening depression. Franklin Delano Roosevelt easily defeated Hoover in the 1932 election by promising to take more vigorous action to restore the nation's economy.

To the Senate and House of Representatives:
The Constitution requires that the President "shall, from time to time, give to the Congress information of the

Speech delivered before the U.S. Congress by Herbert Hoover on December 3, 1929.

124

state of the Union, and recommend to their consideration such measures as he shall judge necessary and expedient." In complying with that requirement I wish to emphasize that during the past year the Nation has continued to grow in strength; our people have advanced in comfort; we have gained in knowledge; the education of youth has been more widely spread; moral and spiritual forces have been maintained; peace has become more assured. The problems with which we are confronted are the problems of growth and of progress. In their solution we have to determine the facts, to develop the relative importance to be assigned to such facts, to formulate a common judgment upon them, and to realize solutions in a spirit of conciliation.

We are not only at peace with all the world, but the foundations for future peace are being substantially strengthened. To promote peace is our long-established policy. Through the Kellogg-Briand pact a great moral standard has been raised in the world. By it fifty-four nations have covenanted to renounce war and to settle all disputes by pacific means. Through it a new world outlook has been inaugurated which has profoundly affected the foreign policies of nations. Since its inauguration we have initiated new efforts not only in the organization of the machinery of peace but also to eliminate dangerous forces which produce controversies amongst nations. . . .

General Economic Situation

The country has enjoyed a large degree of prosperity and sound progress during the past year with a steady improvement in methods of production and distribution and consequent advancement in standards of living. Progress has, of course, been unequal among industries, and some, such as coal, lumber, leather, and textiles, still lag behind. The long upward trend of fundamental progress, however, gave rise to over-optimism as to profits, which translated itself into a wave of uncontrolled speculation in securities, resulting in the diversion of capital from business to the stock market and the inevitable crash. The natural consequences have been a reduction in the consumption of luxuries and semi-necessities by those who have met with losses, and a number of persons thrown temporarily out of employment. Prices of agricultural products dealt in upon the great markets have been affected in sympathy with the stock crash.

Fortunately, the Federal reserve system had taken measures to strengthen the position against the day when speculation would break, which together with the strong position of the banks has carried the whole credit system through the crisis without impairment. The capital which has been hitherto absorbed in stock-market loans for speculative purposes is now returning to the normal channels of business. There has been no inflation in the prices of commodities; there has been no undue accumulation of goods, and foreign trade has expanded to a magnitude which exerts a steadying influence upon activity in industry and employment.

The problems with which we are confronted are the problems of growth and of progress.

The sudden threat of unemployment and especially the recollection of the economic consequences of previous crashes under a much less secured financial system created unwarranted pessimism and fear. It was recalled that past storms of similar character had resulted in retrenchment of construction, reduction of wages, and laying off of workers. The natural result was the tendency of business agencies throughout the country to pause in their plans and proposals for continuation and extension of their business, and this hesitation unchecked could in itself intensify into a depression with widespread unemployment and suffering.

I have, therefore, instituted systematic, voluntary measures of cooperation with the business institutions and with state and municipal authorities to make certain that fundamental businesses of the country shall continue as usual, that wages and therefore consuming power shall not be reduced, and that a special effort shall be made to expand construction work in order to assist in equalizing other deficits in employment. Due to the enlarged sense of cooperation and responsibility which has grown in the business world during the past few years the response has been remarkable and satisfactory. We have canvassed the Federal Government and instituted measures of prudent expansion in such work that should be helpful, and upon which the different departments will make some early recommendations to Congress.

I am convinced that through these measures we have

reestablished confidence. Wages should remain stable. A very large degree of industrial unemployment and suffering which would otherwise have occurred has been prevented. Agricultural prices have reflected the returning confidence. The measures taken must be vigorously pursued until normal conditions are restored.

The agricultural situation is improving. The gross farm income as estimated by the Department of Agriculture for the crop season 1926–27 was $12,100,000,000; for 1927–28 it was $12,300,000,000; for 1928–29 it was $12,500,000,000; and estimated on the basis of prices since the last harvest the value of the 1929–30 crop would be over $12,600,000,000. The slight decline in general commodity prices during the past few years naturally assists the farmers' buying power.

The number of farmer bankruptcies is very materially decreased below previous years. The decline in land values now seems to be arrested and rate of movement from the farm to the city has been reduced. Not all sections of agriculture, of course, have fared equally, and some areas have suffered from drought. Responsible farm leaders have assured me that a large measure of confidence is returning to agriculture and that a feeling of optimism pervades that industry.

The most extensive action for strengthening the agricultural industry ever taken by any government was inaugurated through the farm marketing act of June 15 last. Under its provisions the Federal Farm Board has been established, comprised of men long and widely experienced in agriculture and sponsored by the farm organizations of the country. During its short period of existence the board has taken definite steps toward a more efficient organization of agriculture, toward the elimination of waste in marketing, and toward the upbuilding of farmers' marketing organizations on sounder and more efficient lines. Substantial headway has been made in the organization of four of the basic commodities—grain, cotton, livestock, and wool. Support by the board to cooperative marketing organizations and other board activities undoubtedly have served to steady the farmers' market during the recent crisis and have operated also as a great stimulus to the cooperative organization of agriculture. The problems of the industry are most complex, and the need for sound organization is imperative. Yet the board is moving rapidly along the lines laid out for it in the act, facilitating the creation by farmers of farmer-owned and farmer-controlled organizations and federating them into central institutions, with a view to increasing the bargaining power of agriculture, preventing and controlling surpluses, and mobilizing the economic power of agriculture.

6

Establishing Government Regulations and Safeguards

Gordon V. Axon

In the following excerpt from his book *The Stock Market Crash of 1929*, author Gordon V. Axon reviews the legislative reforms and controls instituted after the crash. As a result of corruption in the financial community, for example, Congress passed the Securities Exchange Act of 1934, which regulated trading on the stock market, giving investors more information and better protection when trading on the stock exchange. Congress also established the Securities and Exchange Commission (SEC) to patrol the activities on Wall Street. According to Axon, the attitude toward government regulation of stock speculation changed as a result of the crash, but the balance between regulation and financial freedom continues to be the subject of debate.

The financial odor out of Wall Street and banking circles filled the nation's air after the 1929 crash, and it grew more putrid as the years passed, the Depression arrived, and banking scandals were disclosed. The Augean stables of finance certainly needed a thorough cleansing. But, as so often happens in history, people are remembered as symbols of a morally bankrupt system, since their crimes were many and various, extending over many years, and far too complex to be fully described here.

Consider, for example, such corrupt titans of finance as

Excerpted from "Effect of the Crash on the Future: Corrective Measures, Laws, and Controls" by Gordon V. Axon in *The Stock Market Crash of 1929* (New York: Mason/Charter, 1974).

Albert H. Wiggin of the Chase National Bank, Charles E. Mitchell of the National City Bank, and Richard Whitney, who for many years had been the president of the New York Stock Exchange. Jesse L. Livermore, gambler extraordinaire, had a book published shortly before he committed suicide; the book was entitled *How to Trade in Stocks*. Dozens of others in business, banking, and the stock market found lasting relief in a leap from a bridge, in poison, or in gassing. (Not that the United States was the only one engulfed in startling revelations of sordid scandal and personal corruption. In Britain, for example, Clarence Hatry, the financier, had been put behind bars in 1930 for issuing stock that did not exist and for sundry other feats of the imagination. The Swedish match king, Ivar Kreuger, preferred a bullet below the heart when his Swedish Match Company was wrecked by speculation and fraud.)

A Need for Reform

A housecleaning was clearly overdue. Neither business nor finance can operate successfully under such corruption. The boom days, of course, had seen deceit successfully hidden under apparent achievements that often were widely applauded. The market crash, the Depression, and the banking collapse revealed only too clearly that many men of financial distinction were men of moral straw.

Financial reform was a must. The sheer magnitude of the stock market crash made strong legislation inevitable. Congress passed such legislation. The Securities Act of 1933 (popularly known as the Truth-in-Securities Act) for example required issuers of stocks and bonds to give much more information than formerly about the securities they were offering to the public. The Banking Act of 1933 made it unlawful for banks to have the notorious "security affiliates" through which stock gambling with bank funds had been possible. The Securities Exchange Act of 1934 regulated stock market trading. This act, along with the Securities Act of 1933, gave investors more information about what they buying; gave them better protection when buying and selling on the stock exchanges; and outlawed such practices as bear raids [in which investors sell borrowed securities in the hope of buying them back at a lower price], and insider transactions that worked against those on the outside, such as the small investor.

These legislative actions were followed by the Public Utility Holding Company Act of 1935, which compelled financial simplicity in a group that had become unbelievably complex in capital structure, as well as operationally.

The Trust Indenture Act of 1939 was passed because quite often the trustee, responsible for protecting the interests of investors, had failed to do so since his loyalties were split between the debtor and the investors. The law required the indenture (document) to specify the rights of the holders of securities such as bonds, and it imposed high standards of conduct on the trustee.

The Investment Company Act of 1940, and the Investment Advisers Act of 1940, regulated the practices of investment companies and the activities of investment advisers.

The securities business became subject to control by the Securities and Exchange Commission (SEC). This was a most important step, in that the regulation of Wall Street had been fought desperately by the aristocrats of finance who believed in the divine right of those with money. In brief, the Securities and Exchange Commission was a policeman provided to patrol the activities of Wall Street. It was to determine the adequacy of data supplied to the public, make rules to help the investor help himself, prevent sellers of securities from making fancy forecasts of future earnings, refuse to accept dubious statements, and, in short, insure minimum standards of behavior. In future, the investor would be allowed to make a fool of himself, but others would find it harder to make him look foolish.

Furthermore, the Federal Reserve Board received authority to fix margin requirements on the trading of securities, making it more difficult for speculation to rise uncontrollably, since investors could be forced to pay a larger deposit—even the full price—when buying securities.

The fact that so many laws had to be passed, and that so much else had to be done, publicly and privately, indicates not only the extent of the dishonesty and chaos but the outrage of an angry people.

The banking structure was cleansed but not healed. Its many weaknesses of structure could not be corrected immediately. However, the Banking Act of 1933 certainly helped assure that, in the future, banks would no longer operate commercial banking along with investment banking. So some banks, such as Chase and National City, disposed of their security affiliates through which they had gambled heavily and lost. The House of Morgan itself was split in two and became a commercial banking house.

A New Attitude

Even more important than what was done to correct immediate abuses was the change in attitude on the part of the American public as well as of those in financial and banking circles.

In 1929, few investors would have thought, or wished, that stock market transactions would soon be closely supervised by a government agency. The crash changed all that.

Too many had lost too much in the stock market débâcle, and too many depositors had seen their banks go out of business entirely, simply closing their doors for good, being legally dissolved and having nothing with which to repay their customers' savings.

Here we see, of course, the constant clash between freedom and regulation. The freedom had proved too heady, so regulation came in the wake of the disaster in stocks and in banks. Later, the early reforms were enhanced and consolidated by further measures that put both banks and securities firms under closer public watch. Likewise, the New York Stock Exchange, still the most important organized stock exchange and then the mainstay of the securities business, changed its own rules and regulations to provide a more professional and orderly market that helped the brokerage houses themselves, as well as investors, since more and more Americans became interested in stock market investing as greater opportunities for secure investments were made available through detailed information and honest trading.

Broader financial questions also must be considered. Because many banks had become bogged down with mortgages that could not be paid off, agencies of the federal government had to be set up to refinance farm and home mortgages. As a result of those actions, the federal government now has an enormous impact on the home-building industry—for instance, with its regulated interest rates, federal guarantees on insured mortgages, and the supply of billions of dollars.

Of greater international and national impact was the devaluation of the dollar. Britain was already off the gold exchange standard when President Roosevelt decided in April

1933 to suspend the convertibility of the dollar into gold and to allow the dollar to float. In January 1934, the fixed price of $35 an ounce for gold became law, in effect devaluing the dollar in terms of gold by about 41 percent.

This inflationary boost helped business and gave the stock market a much needed stimulus, considering the very depressed level of prices. Dollar devaluation and increased government spending were obviously helping the economy.

Today, we take it for granted that the government has control over national economic and financial policies, that bank deposits should be insured and thus secured, that stock operators should not be allowed to fleece the public with impunity, and that banks should not mix banking with gambling in the stock market. The current system, of course, is not perfect and never will be. Abuses still exist and no doubt always will, but the stock market crash of 1929 and the banking fiasco of 1933 made certain that never again would financial circles be operated for the benefit of those with wealth and at the expense of those without.

In the future, the investor would be allowed to make a fool of himself, but others would find it harder to make him look foolish.

We see now, of course, that government regulation can never entirely replace the need for investors to consider carefully where they put their money. Even now, scandals arise in banks and brokerage houses, but they are small compared with those that were accepted as normal in the heady days up to 1929. In those days, an aristocracy of finance existed that viewed almost with contempt the small investor and small depositor, regarding them as fair game in amassing fortunes.

Today, the rich and the poor still exist, but the nation is mainly middle-class, and tens of millions of investors and bank depositors are happily unaware of what went on in the 1920s.

For Further Research

Original Publications

Frederick Lewis Allen, *Only Yesterday: An Informal History of the Nineteen-Twenties*. New York: Perennial Library, 1931.

Anonymous, "Bulls, Bears, and Lambs," *North American Review*, January 1929. Available from University of Northern Iowa, 1222 West 27th St., Cedar Falls, IA, 50614-0516.

Eddie Cantor, *Caught Short!* New York: Simon & Schuster, 1929.

Irving Fisher, *Booms and Depressions, Some First Principles*. New York: Adelphi, 1932.

Garet Garrett, *A Bubble That Broke the World*. Boston: Little, Brown, 1932.

Parker Thomas Moon, ed., *Business, Speculation, and Money: A Series of Addresses and Papers Presented at the Annual Meeting of the Academy of Political Science, November 22, 1929*. New York: Columbia University, 1930.

Alan H. Temple, "The Financial Outlook," *North American Review*, June 1929.

H. Parker Willis, "The Failure of the Federal Reserve," *North American Review*, May 1929.

Barnie F. Winkelman, *Ten Years of Wall Street*. Philadelphia: John C. Winston, 1932.

Books

Gordon V. Axon, *The Stock Market Crash of 1929*. New York: Mason/Charter, 1974.

Harold Bierman Jr., *The Great Myths of 1929 and the Lessons to Be Learned*. Westport, CT: Greenwood Press, 1991.

Edward Chancellor, *Devil Take the Hindmost: A History of Financial Speculation*. New York: Farrar, Straus & Giroux, 1999.

John Kenneth Galbraith, *The Great Crash: 1929*. Boston: Houghton Mifflin, 1979.

S. Marshall Kempner, *Inside Wall Street, 1920–1942*. New York: Hastings House, 1973.

Charles P. Kindleberger, *The World in Depression, 1929–1939*. Berkeley: University of California Press, 1986.

William K. Klingaman, *1929: The Year of the Great Crash*. New York: Harper and Row, 1989.

J.R. Levien, *Anatomy of a Crash, 1929*. New York: Traders Press, 1966.

Michael E. Parrish, *Anxious Decades: America in Prosperity and Depression, 1920–1941*. New York: W.W. Norton, 1992.

Robert Trescott Patterson, *The Great Boom and Panic, 1921–1929*. Chicago: H. Regnery, 1965.

Cabell B.H. Phillips, *From the Crash to the Blitz, 1929–1939*. New York: Macmillan, 1969.

Tom Shachtman, *The Day America Crashed*. New York: G.P. Putnam's Sons, 1979.

Warren Sloat, *1929, America Before the Crash*. New York: Macmillan, 1979.

Robert Sobel, *The Great Bull Market: Wall Street in the 1920s*. New York: W.W. Norton, 1968.

Robert Sobel, *Panic on Wall Street: A History of America's Financial Disasters*. London: Macmillan, 1968.

Antony C. Sutton, *Wall Street and FDR*. New Rochelle, NY: Arlington House, 1975.

Gordon Thomas and Max Morgan-Witts, *The Day the Bubble Burst: A Social History of the Wall Street Crash of 1929*. Garden City, NY: Doubleday, 1979.

Barrie A. Wigmore, *The Crash and Its Aftermath: A History of Securities Markets in the United States, 1929–1933*. Westport, CT: Greenwood Press, 1985.

Periodicals

Economist, "Freedom from Fear?" September 11, 1999.

Amy Feldman, "Papa Abe," *Money*, November 2000.

J.S. Gordon, "The Farthest Fall," *American Heritage*, July/August 1991.

J.S. Gordon, "The Man Who Wasn't There," *American Heritage*, November 1991.

Michael Hirsh, "Banking on a New Order," *Newsweek*, November 1, 1999.

Marci McDonald, "A History of Shopping Binges," *U.S. News & World Report*, May 24, 1999.

Peter Rappoport and Eugene N. White, "Was the Crash of 1929 Expected?" *American Economic Review*, May 1994.

Robert J. Samuelson, "What We Learn from the 1920s," *Newsweek*, February 12, 2001.

Rob Wherry, "Rethinking Raskob," *Forbes*, October 9, 2000.

Eugene N. White, "The Stock Market Boom and Crash of 1929 Revisited," *Journal of Economic Perspectives*, Spring 1990.

Internet Sources

Library of Congress, "Depression and WWII," *America's Story*. www.americaslibrary.gov/egi-bin/page.cgi/jb/1929-1945.

R. Richard Savill, "The Crash of 1929." http://mypage.direct.ca/r/rsavill/Thecrash.html.

Mark Underwood, "Black Thursday: October 24, 1929." http://sac.uky.edu/~msunde00/hon202/p4/nyt.html.

Index

DATE DUE